POPE JOHN PAUL II ON JEWS AND JUDAISM
1979-1986

with Introduction and Commentary

by

Eugene J. Fisher and Leon Klenicki

Editors

This publication
is a joint effort of the
NCCB Committee for Ecumenical
and Interreligious Affairs and the
Anti-Defamation League of
B'nai B'rith

As its September 1986 meeting, the NCCB Committee for Ecumenical and Interreligious Affairs received and approved a recommendation from its Secretariat for Catholic-Jewish Relations to prepare an edition, with commentary, of the numerous addresses of *Pope John Paul II on Jews and Judaism, 1979-1986* in anticipation of the Holy Father's scheduled meeting with American Jewish leaders during his visit to the United States in September 1987. The present document has been prepared by Dr. Eugene Fisher, Executive Secretary of the Secretariat for Catholic-Jewish Relations, in cooperation with Rabbi Leon Klenicki of the Anti-Defamation League of B'nai B'rith, and has been authorized for publication by the undersigned.

Monsignor Daniel F. Hoye
General Secretary
NCCB/USCC

April 24, 1987

ISBN 1-55586-151-2

Contents

Introduction: From Historical Mistrust to Mutual Recognition

For almost two millennia, Christians and Jews have lived in the same universe, under the same sky. They are both in history, experiencing history. But, they have seldom been together. To be in the same place does not necessarily imply togetherness, the sharing of a living presence of the other as a child of God. Although there are eloquent contemporary exceptions, Jews and Christians primarily have seen each other as objects—in many respects, as objects of contempt. The negative opinions of each other have, at times, translated this alienation into an enmity of word and action. Prejudice all too often still shapes the faith commitment, influencing the spiritual encounter and society itself.

This relationship of monologue, of seeing not the other but only one's own construct—or stereotype—of the other, is undergoing a transformation in the last decades of the twentieth century. The focus now is on dialogue, a meeting of hearts, a prophetic encounter of faith. This encounter through dialogue is a reckoning of time past, of deeds, of what has been done and left undone. It is a moment of facing history. True dialogue between Jews and Christians is a process that entails a consideration of each other's faith commitment as part of God's design and way. It demands a critical examination by Christians of their traditional presentation of Jews and Judaism; and by Jews of their attitudes toward Christianity. Dialogue means a reflection on the witnessing of each faith and on the possibility of a joint witness—a witnessing to each other and to the world, which is respectful of each other's differences. Dialogue necessitates a reckoning with centuries of one-sided teaching and centuries of memory. Christians have to overcome 2,000 years of contempt for Israel's covenant with God, for Israel's mission in the world. Jews have to overcome 2,000 years of memories, memories of the crusades, of ghettos, and of the wearing of special garments to identify their Jewish condition. They have to overcome memories of the present as well—memories of widespread Christian silence during, and even complicity in, the Hol-

1

ocaust and with continuing Christian misunderstandings of the State of Israel and of the struggle of Jews for security in their ancient homeland.

Some 2,000 years ago, during the first century in Christian chronology, two divinely appointed vocations were shaped out of a common heritage. It was, as Paul seems to portray it in the Epistle to the Romans, like the relationship between root and branches. The root is the word of God expressed in the Hebrew Bible from the first to the last book; the branches are rabbinic Judaism and Christianity. God's word, especially after the destruction of the temple by Roman troops in the year 70 C.E. (Common Era), was expanded into distinct yet related messages by these two great movements of faith.

Rabbinic Judaism, which developed from Pharisaism, was the in-depth process of understanding God's covenantal relationship after the destruction of the Jerusalem Temple. Rabbinic Judaism built an inner temple that has lasted for centuries. In our time, this inner temple has suffered its greatest challenge by the devastating wind of the *Shoah,* the Holocaust committed by Nazi totalitarianism. The twentieth century marks a new time for Jews searching, once again, for the meaning of God, the presence of God in Jewish existence.

Christianity, the other branch that developed from the root of biblical Israel, expressed itself in the writings of the New Testament and related texts, conveying the mission of Jesus to humanity. Interestingly, it too finds the source of many of its doctrines and rituals in Pharisaic and Synagogue Judaism. Due to the impact of history, both arms of God have been fighting with each other for centuries up to our own days.

Christianity, especially after its alliance with Constantine, the fourth-century Roman emperor, became the established religion of the Roman Empire. That gave to Christian leaders the political power that enabled God's word to be spread through the then-known world. But, it also opened Christians to the corruptive force of power. The alliance of secular power and ecclesiastical power in Christian history meant for the Jewish community numerous restrictions in its civil life. In the late Middle Ages, Jews were ordered to live in special quarters—the ghettos—and were forbidden to exercise the normal work and professions open to other citizens. Jews were forbidden to own or cultivate land or to engage in certain kinds of business activities and were, thus, pressed into the exercise of money-lending, which was not allowed to Christians. Jews were at the mercy of ecclesiastical leaders and secular kings. Often, mobs, incited by sermons and the Christian teaching of contempt—especially, it is sad to say, during

2

Holy Week when the deicide charge would burst forth—would erupt into violence against the Jews.

The theological teaching of contempt accused the Jews of being the killers of Jesus and condemned them to eternal Diaspora. The teaching of contempt disqualified the covenant between God and Israel, arguing that it was superseded by a new covenant—the Christian testimony—with the coming of Jesus. In the Middle Ages, religious confrontations were called to debate theological points. Jews, rabbis and religious teachers, were obligated to explain biblical passages, such as references to Emanuel or to the suffering servant in Isaiah, which Christians saw as typological references to Jesus and his vocation. The confrontations generally ended in expulsion of the Jews from the city, the burning of sacred Hebrew books, or the imposition of more restrictions on the civil rights of the Jewish community.

In modern times, social changes introduced by the Industrial Revolution and modernity somewhat change the picture. Jews were allowed to become citizens, with the same obligations as other citizens but, generally, not with the same advantages. Jews were "tolerated" but never fully accepted into European society. This lack of pluralism, of respect for the other as he or she is, transformed the theological anti-Judaism of Christian teaching into a new dimension. Modern social and racial anti-Semitism is a force that is trying to restrict Jewish rights and threatens the very destruction of the Jewish community. The culmination of modern social anti-Semitism took place with the pagan totalitarianism of Nazi Germany. In a way, anti-Jewish policies of the Soviet Union today can be understood as an extension of this ultimate anti-Semitism.

The Holocaust was a devastating wind that took six million Jews to the gas chamber and to systematic murder. The Holocaust is one of the turning points in Jewish history, but it is also the greatest challenge to Christian commitment. The Holocaust occurred in the very heart of Western Christian civilization and was performed by a nation that had proclaimed for centuries its Christianity, had given to the world great Christian thinkers and theologians as well as the most sophisticated diabolic murderers. The Holocaust entails for the Jewish people a rethinking of Jewish vocation and role in history. It also entails a Christian reckoning of Christian silence, indifference, and complicity, despite the heroic deeds of some Christians in saving Jewish lives.

The twentieth century marks for Jews and Christians a new moment. It is a time of vast spiritual change, of incredible scientific creativity, and of historical development. It is a time of great hope

3

but, equally, a time of profound despair. Persecutions, murder, hunger, lack of sensitivity over the situation of the vast majority of humanity are signs of a failure in our religious witnessing. For Jews and Christians, the twentieth century is the first century in proclaiming together God's covenant. For Jews, it is a rethinking of their commitment vis-à-vis tolerance and the nearly eternal danger of total destruction. Rethinking the meaning of the covenant and God's call signifies a consideration of the diabolic forces that will always attempt to destroy the people of God. Totalitarianism in any form is an attempt to destroy God's covenant.

Christians and Jews are, for the first time, together in history, together to discover for themselves their own proper vocations in a time of radical change. It is a time to look closely at each other, to overcome the teaching of contempt and memories, and to see the other as a part of the covenant of God. It is a new time of reckoning, renewal, and prophetic response.

The Second Vatican Council, in the 1960s, began a period of actualization and active awareness, of experience of God, and of God's presence in the contemporary Christian historical context. It was called *aggiornamento* by Pope John XXIII. The Council initiated in the Church a process of inner renewal that entails respect for the other. Pope John Paul II has played a key role in expounding certain concepts and ideas for further reflection by the Catholic community. Along with the Church's fundamental probing of the mystery of God's people—Israel—two questions require the serious consideration and reflection of the Catholic people of God today. Pope John Paul II has paid attention to both of them. One is the question of anti-Semitism and the Holocaust, and the other is the reality of the State of Israel.

The consideration of anti-Semitism was central to the Second Vatican Council's reckoning with the Jewish people in its declaration *Nostra Aetate* (1965). Its language, however, was seen by many to lack strength. In the words of *Nostra Aetate,* the Church "deplores anti-Semitism." The 1974 *Guidelines and Suggestions for Implementing "Nostra Aetate" (no. 4)* "condemn (as opposed to the very spirit of Christianity) all forms of anti-Semitism." Pope John Paul II has more recently called anti-Semitism "sinful" for all Catholics. In such progressive interpretations, one can see the positive development of church teaching today.

The following commentary and texts, it is hoped, will enable the reader to chart the extraordinary contributions made by Pope John Paul II to the historic dialogue between Jews and Catholics today. The spiritual pilgrimage undertaken by the pope on his way to the

Synagogue of Rome, the first visit ever by a pope to a synagogue since the time of Peter, spanned centuries of mistrust. The story of that pilgrimage, here presented, is, we believe, an exciting one and one filled with profound courage and faith in the future.

Leon Klenicki

Pope John Paul II's Pilgrimage of Reconciliation: A Commentary on the Texts

Through the choice of the name that would mark his pontificate, Pope John Paul II paid homage and made a commitment to all three of his immediate predecessors: John XXIII, who called the Second Vatican Council and who mandated that it address the ancient, long-neglected question of the Church's spiritual debt to Judaism; Paul VI, who implemented that mandate and who institutionalized it through the creation of the Holy See's Commission for Religious Relations with the Jews; and John Paul I, the "smiling pope," whose all too brief reign was marked by an appreciation for the "divine humor" of creation and a sense of abiding hope in humanity.

The declaration on the Jews, *Nostra Aetate,* 4, distilled in fifteen tightly worded Latin sentences the essence of the Second Vatican Council's major themes of biblical reappraisal, liturgical renewal, and openness to the Spirit working in the world beyond the visible boundaries of the Church. Implementation of *Nostra Aetate,* then, can properly be seen as a "litmus test" for the success or failure of the Council's vision as a whole. How has Pope John Paul II fulfilled his commitment to his predecessors in the area of Catholic-Jewish relations, the area of the Church's ministry that embodies the most ancient and, some would say, potentially divisive issues posed to the Church by its own history?

The following addresses and remarks by the pope were given on numerous occasions and in a remarkably wide range of locations throughout the world. Virtually wherever the pope has travelled, it can be said, there exists a Jewish community, whether large, as in the United States, or tragically small, as in the tiny remnant of the once-flourishing Jewish community of Poland. And, wherever the pope goes, he seeks out those communities to reach out to them in reconciliation and affirmation of the infinite worth of Judaism's continuing proclamation of the name of the One God in the world.

7

The papal talks included here represent all those that have been officially printed. They provide a record of a profound spiritual pilgrimage for the pope and the Church, almost two millennia after the Church's birth as a Jewish movement in the land and among the people of Israel. They are ordered in this book chronologically rather than thematically. For, as we will try to show in the thematic analysis that follows, if read carefully, one can discern in them a growth and development in the pope's understanding of and appreciation for how "the Jews define themselves in the light of their own religious experience" (Prologue, 1974 *Guidelines,* cited by the pope in his first address to representatives of Jewish organizations, 3/12/79).* Perhaps more important, this development teaches us much about how the Church must reinterpret today its own understanding of its relationship to the Jewish people as "people of God."

The ongoing papal reconsideration and redefinition of ancient theological categories represent the fruits of a painstaking effort, supported by the efforts of thousands of Catholics and Jews in dialogue throughout the world, as the pope has acknowledged (Historic Visit to the Synagogue of Rome, 4/13/86, no. 4), to articulate anew the mystery of the Church in the light of a positive articulation of the abiding mystery of Israel. The results, as the patient reader will discern, are as breathtaking as they have been painstaking.

Progress, in one sense, has been painfully slow since the Second Vatican Council. It is measured in small steps, a word here uttered to clarify an awkward phrase there; a slightly less ambiguous wording to replace a more ambiguous, potentially misleading theological formula; and so forth. But, the direction is clear, we believe, and the basic message starkly unambiguous: the Church is not alone in the world as "people of God." The Church is joined by the Jewish people in its proclamation of the oneness of God and the true nature of human history, which is defined by its end, the coming Reign of God for which Jews and Christians alike pray daily and, through their prayers, proclaim universally (cf. 1985 Vatican "Notes," II, 9–11). The following thematic categories serve to organize just some of these

---

* The papal addresses cited in this commentary are referred to by the dates on which they were delivered. For a complete listing of titles and chronological order, see Contents in this publication.

small steps and interventions by which the pope has sought to frame and to move forward the Church's side of historic dialogue between Catholics and Jews.

In assessing the major events of the year 1986 in the Diocese of Rome, the pope singled out his visit to "our elder brothers in the faith of Abraham in their Rome Synagogue" as his most significant action of the year. It will be remembered, he predicted, "for centuries and millenniums in the history of this city and this Church. I thank Divine Providence because the task was given to me" (*National Catholic News Service,* 12/31/86).

1. The Spiritual Bond between the Church and the Jewish People: The Special Relationship

The notion of a "spiritual bond" linking the Church and the Jewish people ("Abraham's stock") was central to *Nostra Aetate.* It has become a major theme of Pope John Paul II's own reflections on the subject over the years, one which he has consistently tried to probe and refine. In his first address to Jewish representatives, for example, he interpreted the conciliar phrase as meaning "that our two religious communities are connected and closely related at the very level of their respective identities" (3/12/79) and spoke of "fraternal dialogue" between the two.

Terms such as *fraternal* and addressing one another as *brothers* and *sisters,* of course, reflect ancient usage *within* the Christian community. They imply an acknowledgment of a commonality of faith, with liturgical implications. It was an ecumenical breakthrough, for example, when the Second Vatican Council and Pope Paul VI began the practice of addressing Orthodox and Protestant Christians in such terms. Pope John Paul II's extension of this terminology to Jews, therefore, is by no means accidental.

The relationship, he is saying, is not marginal to the Church. Rather, it reaches to the very essence of the nature of Christian faith itself, so that to deny it is to deny something essential to the teaching of the Church (cf. Vatican "Notes," I, 2). The spiritual bond with Jews, for the pope, is properly understood as a "sacred one, stemming as it does from the mysterious will of God" (10/28/85).

In bringing this lesson home, the pope has used startling and powerful language. In his important allocution to the Jewish community of Mainz, W. Germany (11/17/80), for example, the pope likened

9

the relationship to that between "the first and second part" of the Christian Bible (i.e., between the Hebrew Scriptures and the New Testament).

The dialogue between Catholics and Jews, therefore, is not a dialogue between past (Judaism) and present (Christianity) realities, as if the former had been "superseded" or "replaced" by the latter, as certain Christian polemicists would have it. "On the contrary," the pope made clear in Mainz, "it is a question rather of reciprocal enlightenment and explanation, just as is the relationship between the Scriptures themselves" (cf. *Dei Verbum*, 11).

In this vein, the pope has also moved to assist Catholics to formulate more sensitive biblical terminology. Instead of the traditional terms *Old Testament* and *New Testament*, which might be understood to imply that the "old" has been abrogated in favor of the "new" (a false conclusion known from history as the Marcionite heresy), the pope, in his recent address to the Jews of Australia (11/26/86), has suggested the use of the terms, the *Hebrew Scriptures* and the *Christian Scriptures* as appropriate alternatives. Again, small changes can have major consequences in theological and sociological perception.

In the pope's view, so close is the spiritual bond between our two "peoples of God" that the dialogue is properly considered—unlike any other relationship between the Church and a world religion—to be "a dialogue within our Church" (Mainz, 11/17/80). Interpreting *Nostra Aetate* during his visit to the Rome Synagogue, the pope brought these themes to a dramatic culmination:

> The Church of Christ discovers her "bond" with Judaism by "searching into her own mystery" (*Nostra Aetate*, 4). The Jewish religion is not "extrinsic" to us, but in a certain way is "intrinsic" to our own religion. With Judaism, therefore, we have a relationship which we do not have with any other religion. You are dearly beloved brothers and, in a certain way, it could be said that you are our elder brothers (Rome, 4/13/86).

2. A Living Heritage

The phrase, "elder brothers," used here with caution, raises the question of how the pope has dealt with the sometimes awkward (for Christians) question of the Church's spiritual debt to Judaism. Traditionally, this debt has been acknowledged—as in medieval canon law's exception allowing Jews freedom of worship (within certain

10

limitations)—a right granted to no other religious group outside Christianity.

Yet, the acknowledgment often came negatively. For many Christians over the ages, for example, the use of the term *elder brother* applied to the Jews would have conjured images of apologetic interpretations of the younger/elder brother stories of Genesis in which the younger brother takes over the heritage or *patrimony* of the elder (e.g., Esau and Jacob). The powerful imagery of the gothic cathedrals of Europe is another example of this. Juxtaposed on either side of the portals of many medieval cathedrals is a statue of the Synagogue (portrayed in the physical form of a woman), her head bowed, holding a broken staff of the law, with the tablets of the Ten Commandments slipping from her fingers, on the one side, and the Church, resplendently erect and triumphant on the other. The pairings symbolized for the medieval artists the passage of the Covenant from Judaism to Christianity.

Here, as in so many other ways, however, the pope has sought to reinterpret ancient apologetics and to replace negative images with positive affirmations. In his address to the Jewish community in Mainz, the pope cited a passage from a declaration of the Bishops of the Federal Republic of Germany, issued earlier that year, calling attention to "the spiritual heritage of Israel for the Church." He added to the citation, however, a single word that removed any possible ambiguity and opened up a new area of theological reflection, calling it "a *living* heritage, which must be understood and preserved in its depth and richness by us Catholic Christians" (11/17/80).

Speaking to delegates from episcopal conferences, gathered in Rome in March 1982, from around the world to discuss ways to foster improved Catholic-Jewish relations, the pope confirmed and advanced this direction of his thought:

> Christians have taken the right path, that of justice and brotherhood, in seeking to come together with their Semitic brethren, respectfully and perseveringly, in the *common* heritage, a heritage that all value so highly. . . . To assess it carefully in itself and with due awareness of the faith and religious life of the Jewish people *as they are professed and practised still today,* can greatly help us to understand better certain aspects of the life of the Church ([3/6/82], italics added).

The "common spiritual patrimony" of Jews and Christians, then, is not something of the past but of the present. Just as the Church,

11

through the writings of its doctors and saints and the statements of its councils, has developed a rich tradition interpreting and clarifying its spiritual heritage over the centuries, so has Judaism developed, through rabbinic literature and the Talmud, through Jewish philosophers and mystics, what was given to it in its founding by God, as the 1985 Vatican "Notes" explicitly state (Section VI). Today, then, the pope calls us to understand the "common spiritual patrimony" not only positively but assertively as a joint witness of God's truth to the world: "Jews and Christians are the trustees and witnesses of an ethic marked by the Ten Commandments in the observance of which man finds his truth and freedom" (Rome Synagogue, 4/13/86). In the perspective of this renewed papal vision, one can imagine a new statue of the Synagogue on cathedrals, head held high in faithful observance of God's perduring law; and a new statue of the Church, with a look of saving humility mitigating the triumphal expression of the past. The two, while remaining distinct, would stand together to proclaim the divine truth that both share and, yet, interpret in unique ways.

3. Permanent Validity of God's Covenant with the Jewish People

Underlying the above considerations is a central message that Pope John Paul II has made his own wherever he has travelled. This message grows out of the Second Vatican Council, and what the pope has done is to make explicit what was implicit in the Council's teaching. Not only *Nostra Aetate* but the Dogmatic Constitution on the Church, *Lumen Gentium,* drew upon the strong affirmation of St. Paul in Romans 11:28–29 when seeking to define the role of the Jewish people in God's plan of salvation, even after the time of Christ: "On account of their fathers, this people [the Jews] remains most dear to God, for God does not repent of the gifts He makes nor of the calls He issues" (*Lumen Gentium,* 16).

Logically, the conciliar affirmation means that Jews remain God's chosen people in the fullest sense ("most dear"). This affirmation, the pope teaches, is unequivocal and in no way diminishes the Church's own affirmation of its own standing as "people of God." In Mainz, the pope addressed the Jewish community with full respect as "the people of God of the Old Covenant, which has never been revoked by God," referring to Romans 11:29, and emphasized the "permanent value" of both the Hebrew Scriptures and the Jewish community that witnesses to those Scriptures as sacred texts (11/17/80).

In meeting with representatives of episcopal conferences, the pope stressed the present tense of Romans 9:4–5 concerning the Jewish people, "who have the adoption as sons, and the glory and the covenants and the legislation and the worship and the promises" (3/6/82), while also affirming "the universal salvific significance of the death and resurrection of Jesus of Nazareth" (ibid.). The pope does not seek a superficial reconciling of these two great truths but affirms them both together, commenting: "this means that the links between the Church and the Jewish people are founded on the design of the God of the Covenant" (ibid.). Or, as the pope put it in addressing the Anti-Defamation League of B'nai B'rith, "the respect we speak of is based on the mysterious spiritual link which brings us close together, in Abraham and, through Abraham, in God who chose Israel and brought forth the Church from Israel" (3/22/84).

Here, there is not the slightest hint of supersessionism or of that subtler form of triumphalism that would envision Israel as having exhausted its salvific role in "giving birth" to Christianity. The mystery, in the pope's profound vision, lies much deeper than any such "either/or" theological dichotomies can reach. It is precisely such a "both/and" approach that the pope is calling Catholic scholars and educators to develop today. In the words of the "Ecumenical Aids" for the Diocese of Rome, the mystery (a term reserved for the sacraments and the deepest truths of the Catholic faith) encompasses "the people of God, Jews and Christians."

The pope's remarkable formulation in Australia distills years of theological development: "The Catholic faith is rooted in the eternal truths of the Hebrew Scriptures and in the irrevocable covenant made with Abraham. We, too, gratefully hold these same truths of our Jewish heritage and look upon you as our brothers and sisters in the Lord" (11/26/86).

4. Catechetics and Liturgy

For the pope, it is not enough to rework the framework of Christianity's traditional understanding of Jews and Judaism. The renewed vision of the relationship needs to permeate every area of church life. In his address to representatives of bishops' conferences, for example, the pope stressed especially, "the case of [Catholic] liturgy, whose Jewish roots remain still to be examined in depth, and in any case should be known and appreciated by our faithful" (3/6/82). Regarding catechesis, he encouraged a major effort: "We should aim, in this field, that Catholic teaching at its different levels, in catechesis to children and young people, presents Jews and Judaism, not only in an honest and objective manner, free from prejudices and without any offenses, but also with full awareness of the heritage sketched above" (ibid.).

In his response to the International Conference of Christians and Jews, the pope noted that the "great common spiritual patrimony" shared by Jews and Christians rests on a "solid" foundation of "faith in a God . . . as a loving father . . .; in a common basic liturgical pattern, and in a common commitment, grounded in faith, to all men and women in need, who are our 'neighbors' (cf. Lv 19:18, Mk 12:32 and parallels)" (7/6/84). Catechesis and the liturgy itself, in other words, have as a primary goal making clear the "spiritual bond" that links the Church to the people Israel (cf. Vatican "Notes," II, VI).

Also needing to be made clear to Catholic youth is the often tragic history of Christian-Jewish relations over the centuries: "The proper teaching of history is also a concern of yours [ICCJ's]. Such a concern is very understandable, given the sad and entangled common history of Jews and Christians—a history that is not always taught or transmitted correctly" (7/6/84). As Fr. Edward Flannery commented in his classic study of that history, *The Anguish of the Jews* (Paulist, 1985), "those pages of history that Jews have committed to memory are the very ones that have been torn from Christian history books" (p. 1).

Finally, in his visit to the Rome Synagogue, the pope added a note of urgency and even impatience to his encouragement to Catholic educators and homilists "to present always and everywhere, to ourselves and others, the true face of the Jews and of Judaism . . . at every level of outlook, teaching, and communication" (4/13/86), reminding "my brothers and sisters of the Catholic Church" that guidelines "are already available to everyone." In the 1974 *Guidelines for the Implementation of "Nostra Aetate" (no. 4)*, and in the 1985 "Notes" issued by the Holy See's Commission for Religious Relations with Judaism, the pope concluded that "it is only a question of studying them carefully, of immersing oneself in their teachings, and of putting them into practices" (4/13/86).

5. Condemnations of Anti-Semitism and Remembrances of the *Shoah*

A major theme that runs through the following addresses is the pope's deep abhorrence of anti-Semitism. This abhorrence is not simply theoretical. The pope lived under Nazism in Poland and experienced

14

personally the malignancy of the ancient evil of Jew-hatred.

In his very first audience with Jewish representatives, the pope reaffirmed the Second Vatican Council's repudiation of anti-Semitism "as opposed to the very spirit of Christianity," and "which in any case the dignity of the human person alone would suffice to condemn" (3/12/79). The pope has repeated this message in country after country throughout the world.

And, in country after country, especially in Europe, the pope has called on Catholics to remember, "in particular, the memory of the people whose sons and daughters were intended for total extermination" (Homily at Auschwitz, 6/7/79). From the intensity of his own experience, the pope is able to articulate both the *uniqueness* of the Jewish experience of the *Shoah* (Holocaust) while, at the same time, revering the memory of all of Nazism's millions of non-Jewish victims. He would, it may be appropriate to say, agree unreservedly with the formulation of Elie Wiesel: "Not every victim of the Holocaust was a Jew, but every Jew was a victim."

Meeting with Jews in Paris (5/31/80), the pope made a point of mentioning the great suffering of the Jewish community of France "during the dark years of the occupation," paying homage to them as victims "whose sacrifice, we know, has not been fruitless." The pope went on to acknowledge that from the French Jewish survivors came the courage of "pioneers, including Jules Isaac" to engage in the dialogue with Catholics that led to *Nostra Aetate*. In Germany (11/17/80), the pope addressed the subject at some length. And, in his controversial homily at Otranto, he linked, for the first time, the Holocaust and the rebirth of a Jewish State in the land of Israel: "the Jewish People, after tragic experiences connected with the extermination of so many sons and daughters, driven by the desire for security, set up the State of Israel" (10/5/80, see below).

Speaking as a Pole and as a Catholic on the fortieth anniversary of the uprising and destruction of the Warsaw Ghetto, the pope termed "that horrible and tragic event" a "desperate cry for the right to life, for liberty, and for the salvation of human dignity" (4/25/83). On the twentieth anniversary of *Nostra Aetate,* the pope stated that "anti-Semitism, in its ugly and sometimes violent manifestations, should be completely eradicated." He called the attention of the whole Church to the mandate given in the 1985 Vatican "Notes" to develop Holocaust curricula in Catholic schools and catechetical programs: "For Catholics, as the 'Notes' (no. 25) have asked them to do, to fathom the depths of the extermination of many millions of Jews during World War II and the wounds thereby inflicted on the consciousness of the Jewish people, theological reflection is also needed" (10/28/85).

In Australia, the pope recalled that "this is still the century of the *Shoah*" and praised the role Australia played in giving asylum "to thousands of refugees and survivors from that ghastly series of events." He intensified the Council's condemnation of anti-Semitism by declaring that "no theological justification could ever be found for acts of discrimination or persecution against Jews. In fact, such acts must be held to be sinful" (11/26/86).

While not included in full here, it should be noted that over the years the pope has issued strong statements of condemnation of acts of terrorism against synagogues and Jewish communities, sending messages of sympathy for their victims. For example, he condemned the August 29, 1981, bomb-throwing attack on a synagogue in Vienna, Austria as a "bloody and absurd act, which assails the Jewish community in Austria and the entire world," and warned against a "new wave of that same anti-Semitism that has provoked so much mourning through the centuries" (NC News 9/1/81).

During the October 7, 1985, seizure by Palestinian terrorists of the Italian cruise ship Achille Lauro, the pope condemned what he called "this grave act of violence against innocent and defenseless persons," calling on the hijackers to "put an end to their deed": "It is not through recourse to violence that one finds a just solution to problems. I wish that the perpetrators of this rash act would understand this."

After the September 1986 attack on the Istanbul Synagogue, the pope expressed his "firm and vigorous condemnation" of the act and his "heartfelt thought to the victims . . . brothers gathered together in a place of prayer" (*L'Osservatore Romano,* 9/22/86).

6. Land and State of Israel

Because of the great complexities of the Middle East situation, which it is not within the purview of this volume to address, much less unravel, it must be acknowledged that papal teaching on this subject of such central concern to the Jewish community is more nuanced and, at times, ambiguous than that to be found in the other categories included in this analysis. Still, from the perspective of Catholic-Jewish dialogue, which is to say from the perspective of how well Catholics, through dialogue, have come to understand "by what essential traits the Jews define themselves in the light of their own religious experience" (1974 *Guidelines,* Prologue), one can discern a measure of progress in understanding as reflected in the papal statements.

Clearly, there still exist differences of view between the Holy See and the State of Israel, such that the hope for an exchange of ambassadors between the two expressed by many Jewish and Catholic leaders has not yet been realized. The reasons, as stated by the Holy See, include the unsettled nature of the boundary between Israel and some of its neighbors, the disposition of the city of Jerusalem, and the security of Christian communities in Arab countries.

There are, however, certain diplomatic relations between the Holy See and Jerusalem. The Israeli Embassy in Rome includes an officer that relates to the Vatican Secretariat of State. The Apostolic Delegate in Jerusalem communicates with the Israeli Ministry of Foreign Affairs. When Israeli leaders meet with the pope, the protocol is that accorded to a state visit. Given the symbolic as well as practical nature of diplomatic relations, a full exchange of ambassadors would deepen greatly the relationship between Catholics and Jews.

The papal addresses included here represent something of the pope's own generally positive attitudes toward the State of Israel as well as toward the Palestinians and, above all, his very deep hopes that the holy city of Jerusalem can become "a crossroads of reconciliation and peace," a "meeting point" between Christians, Jews, and Muslims (Homily at Otranto, 10/5/80).

The pope's attitude toward the State of Israel is most completely revealed in his Apostolic Letter of April 20, 1984, *Redemptionis Anno:*

> For the Jewish people who live in the State of Israel and who preserve in that land such precious testimonies of their history and their faith, we must ask for the desired security and the due tranquility that is the prerogative of every nation and condition of life and of progress for every society.

This is an unambiguous affirmation of the right of the Jewish State to existence and security.

The Holy See's 1985 "Notes" distinguish between the people, land, and State of Israel. They affirm the validity of the Jewish people's attachment to the land and the existence of the State under international law, but caution against a biblical-fundamentalist interpretation of the religious implications of modern events. While not a papal statement, as such, the reference in the "Notes" deserves to be cited here in full for the overall perspective it gives on the issue as it is raised in Catholic teaching today:

> The history of Israel did not end in A.D. 70 (c.f. *Guidelines,* II).
> It continued, especially in a numerous Diaspora which allowed

Israel to carry to the whole world a witness—often heroic—of its fidelity to the one God and to "exalt him in the presence of all the living" (Tb 13:4), while preserving the memory of the land of their forefathers at the heart of their hope (Passover *Seder*).

Christians are invited to understand this religious attachment, which finds its roots in biblical tradition, without, however, making their own any particular religious interpretation of this relationship (cf. *Statement on Catholic-Jewish Relations,* National Conference of Catholic Bishops, November 20, 1975).

The existence of the State of Israel and its political options should be envisaged not in a perspective which is in itself religious, but in their reference to the common principles of international law (*Notes on the Correct Way to Present Jews and Judaism in the Preaching and Catechesis of the Roman Catholic Church,* Vatican Commission for Religious Relations with the Jews, May 1985).

7. A Vision for the Future: The Call to Joint Witness and Action in History

Central to the pope's vision of the Christian-Jewish relationship is the hope that it offers for joint social action and witness to the One God and the reality of the Kingdom of God as the defining-point of human history. In his address in Mainz, the pope calls this "third dimension" of the dialogue a "sacred duty": "Jews and Christians, as children of Abraham, are called to be a blessing for the world (cf. Gn 12:2ff) by committing themselves to work together for peace and justice among all peoples" (11/17/80).

Such joint action, for the pope, is far more than simple "good neighborliness." It is a fulfillment of what is essential to the mission of both Judaism and Christianity for, "certainly, the great task of promoting justice and peace (cf. Ps 85:4), the sign of the messianic age in both the Jewish and Christian traditions, is grounded in its turn in the great prophetic heritage" (3/22/84). The possibility of a joint proclamation by word and deed in the world, which yet avoids "any syncretism and any ambiguous appropriation" (4/13/86), is seen by the pope as no less than a divine call: "The existence and providence of the Lord, our Creator and Saviour, are thus made present in the witness of our daily conduct and belief. This is one of the responses that those who believe in God and are prepared to 'sanctify his name' [*Kiddush ha-Shem*] (cf. Mt 6:9) can and should give to the secularistic climate of the present day" (4/19/85).

This way of collaboration "in service of humanity" as a means of preparing for God's Kingdom unites Jews and Christians on a level that, in a sense, can be said to be deeper than the doctrinal distinctions that divide us historically. "Through different but finally convergent ways we will be able to reach, with the help of the Lord, who has never ceased to love his people (Rom 11:1), true brotherhood in reconciliation and respect and to contribute to a full implementation of God's plan in history" (3/6/82). That "full implementation" the pope defines in religious terms. It is a "society . . . where justice reigns and where . . . throughout the world it is peace that rules, the *shalom* hoped for by the lawmakers, prophets, and wise men of Israel" (4/13/86).

In conclusion, to use the words of the 1985 Vatican "Notes" to summarize Pope John Paul II's thoughts on Christian-Jewish relations, one can say that it is his vision that through dialogue:

> We shall reach a greater awareness that the people of God of the Ancient [Hebrew] Scriptures and the New Testament are tending toward a like end in the future: the coming or return of the Messiah—even if they start from two different points of view. Attentive to the same God who has spoken, hanging on the same word, we have to witness to one same memory and one common hope in Him who is the master of history. We must also accept our responsibility to prepare the world for the coming of the Messiah by working together for social justice, respect for the rights of persons and nations, and for social and international reconciliation. To this we are driven, Jews and Christians, by the command to love our neighbor, by a common hope for the Kingdom of God, and by the great heritage of the Prophets.

Eugene J. Fisher

1979

Audience for Representatives of Jewish Organizations

March 12, 1979

Jewish Perspectives on Dialogue

On March 12, 1979, Pope John Paul II received in audience representatives of Jewish organizations. They were in Rome for meetings of the International Jewish Liaison Committee. Philip Klutznick, president of the World Jewish Congress, spoke in behalf of the Jewish delegation on that occasion. In the address which follows, he said that the pope had developed a special understanding during World War II of the demonic consequences of hatred directed to the Jews in Poland. He also discussed the problem of Soviet Jewry and the importance of "the covenant of the land" to Jewish people.

"Peace, peace be unto you, and peace be to your helpers" (1 Chr 12:18).

With these words from holy scripture we convey to you our sincere good wishes for the success of your pontificate and offer our heartfelt prayers for the welfare of the millions of Catholic faithful throughout the world.

This is an important occasion in the long and often difficult history of the relations between the Catholic Church and the Jewish people. This history was profoundly affected by Vatican Council II and by subsequent events.

With *Nostra Aetate,* promulgated by the Vatican Council in 1965, and the guidelines of 1975 which amplified the teachings of the conciliar document, the church embarked on a profound examination of its relationship to Judaism. The establishment of the Commission for Religious Relations with the Jews and the formation of the International Catholic-Jewish Liaison Committee served to encourage a fraternal dialogue based on mutual respect. The result has been a significant improvement in Catholic-Jewish understanding and friendship, based on the affirmation of a shared reverence for sacred scripture, the condemnation of anti-Semitism, support of religious liberty and joint social action.

Judaism and the Catholic Church share in the belief that authentic faith compels religious people to be vitally concerned for the welfare of individuals and societies. God is not indifferent to man's injustice toward his fellow man. We have noted with admiration that in areas of the world where grave violations of religious liberty and of other human rights exist, the Catholic Church has courageously upheld the values which flow from our common conviction that human beings are not accidental appearances on the cosmic scene but creations of God whose dignity stems from the divine image implanted by the creator. As a people that has known suffering, and impelled by the moral teachings of our faith, we are committed to the alleviation of human misery and injustice wherever they may be found.

Your Holiness, Poland, your country of origin, was a great center of Jewish culture for over a thousand years. This great epoch in Jewish history came to a tragic end during World War II when most of European Jewry was destroyed, victims of the most virulent anti-Semitism. Your Holiness experienced firsthand the demonic consequences of religious and racial hatred which resulted in the immense human suffering of World War II and culminated in the holocaust of European Jewry. Therefore, you have a special understanding of the importance of eradicating the spiritual sickness that is anti-Semitism and of combating prejudice in all its forms.

Anti-semitism is a disease which can be dormant and then reappear in new and insidious guises. That is why the Jewish community has been so concerned with the problem of Soviet Jewry.

We dedicate ourselves again to the struggle for human rights and fundamental freedoms for all persons and to the cause of religious liberty. Jews will work together with Catholics and others in the common search for social justice and peace.

The guidelines implementing *Nostra Aetate* invite Christians to learn by what essential traits Jews define themselves in the light of their religious experience. In the Jewish self-understanding, the bond of people of the covenant to the land is fundamental. In the long history of the Jewish people, few events have been experienced with as much pain as the Exile, the separation of the people from the land promised by God. Never, during this separation, have the people of Israel lost hope in the fulfillment of the divine promise.

Much progress in the relations of the Catholic Church and the Jewish people has been made since Vatican Council II.

At meetings of the liaison committee we have welcomed the progressive elimination of references unfavorable to Jews and Judaism from Catholic teaching materials and the removal of unfavorable stereotypes from Jewish teaching materials.

We trust that during your pontificate these principles will be reaffirmed and further progress will be made in advancing mutual esteem between our faith communities.

The members of the International Jewish Committee for Interreligious Consultations—consisting of the World Jewish Congress, the Synagogue Council of America, including the Union of American Hebrew Congregations, the American Jewish Committee, the Anti-Defamation League B'nai B'rith—and the Israel Jewish Council for Interreligious Consultations—reiterate their good wishes for the success of the tasks before you. May we together contribute to the world of which Isaiah (32:16–17) spoke when he said:

> Then justice will dwell in the wilderness and righteousness abide in the fruitful field. And the effect of righteousness will be peace, and the result of righteousness quietness and trust forever.

Response of the Pope

In the address which he delivered at this meeting, the pope spoke of fraternal dialogue and collaboration with the Jews and pledged to do everything in his power for the peace of that land "which is holy for you as for us."

Dear Friends,

It is with great pleasure that I greet you, presidents and representatives of the Jewish world organizations, and in that capacity forming with the representatives of the Catholic Church the international liaison committee. I greet also the other representatives of various national Jewish committees who are here with you. Four years ago, my predecessor, Paul VI, received in audience this same international committee and told them how he rejoiced that they had decided to meet in Rome, the city which is the center of the Catholic Church (cf. *Address* of Jan. 10, 1975).

Now you have also decided to come to Rome, to greet the new pope, to meet with members of the Commission for Religious Relations with the Jews, and thus to renew and give a fresh impulse to the dialogue which for the past years you have had with authorized representatives of the Catholic Church. This is indeed, therefore, an important moment in the history of our relations, and I am happy to have the occasion to say a word myself on this subject.

As your representative has mentioned, it was the Second Vatican Council with its declaration *Nostra Aetate* (n. 4) that provided the starting point for this new and promising phase in the relationship between the Catholic Church and the Jewish religious community. In effect, the council made very clear that, "while searching into the mystery of the church," it recalled "the spiritual bond linking the people of the new covenant with Abraham's stock" (*Nostra Aetate,* 4). Thus it understood that our two religious communities are connected and closely related at the very level of their respective religious identities. For "the beginning of [the church's] faith and election are already found among the patriarchs, Moses and the prophets," and "therefore she cannot forget that she received the revelation of the Old Testament through the people with whom God in his inexpressible mercy deigned to establish the ancient covenant" (ibid.). It is on the basis of all this that we recognize with utmost clarity that the path along which we should proceed with the Jewish religious community is one of fraternal dialogue and fruitful collaboration.

According to this solemn mandate, the Holy See has sought to provide the instruments for such dialogue and collaboration and to foster their realization both here at the center and elsewhere throughout the church. Thus, the Commission for Religious Relations with the Jews was created in 1974. At the same time, the dialogue began to develop at several levels in the local churches around the world and with the Holy See itself. I wish to acknowledge here the friendly response and good will, indeed the cordial initiative, that the church has found and continues to find among your organizations and other large sections of the Jewish community.

I believe that both sides must continue their strong efforts to overcome the difficulties of the past, so as to fulfill God's commandment of love, and to sustain a truly fruitful and fraternal dialogue that contributes to the good of each of the partners involved and to our better service of humanity.

The guidelines you have mentioned, whose value I wish to underline and reaffirm, indicate some ways and means to obtain these aims. You have rightly wished to stress a point of particular importance: "Christians must therefore strive to acquire a better knowledge of the basic components of the religious tradition of Judaism; they must strive to learn by what essential traits the Jews define themselves in the light of their own religious experience" (Prologue, *Guidelines and Suggestions for Jewish-Christian Relations,* Vatican Commission for

Religious Relations with the Jews, Dec. 1, 1974). Another important reflection is the following: "In virtue of her divine mission, and her very nature, the church must preach Jesus Christ to the world (*Ad Gentes*, 2). Lest the witness of Catholics to Jesus Christ should give offense to Jews, they must take care to live and spread their Christian faith while maintaining the strictest respect for religious liberty in line with the teaching of the Second Vatican Council (*Dignitatis Humanae*). They will likewise strive to understand the difficulties which arise for the Jewish soul—rightly imbued with an extremely high, pure notion of the divine transcendence—when faced with the mystery of the incarnate Word" (*Guidelines*, 1).

These recommendations refer, of course, to the Catholic faithful, but I do not think it is superfluous to repeat them here. They help us to have a clear notion of Judaism and Christianity and of their true mutual relationship. You are here, I believe, to help us in our reflections on Judaism. And I am sure that we find in you, and in the communities you represent, a real and deep disposition to understand Christianity and the Catholic Church in its proper identity today, so that we may work from both sides toward our common aim of overcoming every kind of prejudice and discrimination.

In this connection it is useful to refer once more to the council declaration *Nostra Aetate* and to repeat what the guidelines say about the repudiation of "all forms of anti-Semitism and discrimination," "as opposed to the very spirit of Christianity," but "which in any case the dignity of the human person alone would suffice to condemn" (*Guidelines*, prologue). The Catholic Church therefore clearly repudiates in principle and in practice all such violations of human rights wherever they may occur throughout the world. I am, moreover, happy to evoke in your presence today the dedicated and effective work of my predecessor Pius XII on behalf of the Jewish people. And on my part I shall continue with divine help in my pastoral ministry in Rome—as I endeavored to do in the See of Cracow—to be of assistance to all who suffer or are oppressed in any way.

Following also in particular in the footsteps of Paul VI, I intend to foster spiritual dialogue and to do everything in my power for the peace of that land which is holy for you as it is for us, with the hope that the city of Jerusalem will be effectively guaranteed as a center of harmony for the followers of the three great monotheistic religions of Judaism, Islam and Christianity, for whom the city is a revered place of devotion.

I am sure that the very fact of this meeting today, which you have so kindly asked to have, is in itself an expression of dialogue and a new step toward that fuller mutual understanding which we are called to achieve. By pursuing this goal we are all sure of being faithful and obedient to the will of God, the God of the patriarchs and prophets. To God, then, I would like to turn at the end of these reflections. All of us, Jews and Christians, pray frequently to him with the same prayers, taken from the Book which we both consider to be the word of God. It is for him to give to both religious communities, so near to each other, that reconciliation and effective love which are at the same time his command and his gift (cf. Lv 19:18; Mk 12:30). In this sense, I believe, each time that Jews recite the "Shema' Israel," each time that Christians recall the first and second great commandments, we are, by God's grace, brought nearer to each other.

As a sign of the understanding and fraternal love already achieved, let me express again my cordial welcome and greetings to you all with that word so rich in meaning, taken from the Hebrew language, which we Christians also use in our Liturgy: Peace be with you. *Shalom. Shalom!*

Homily at Auschwitz

June 7, 1979

Two former Nazi concentration camps were the setting for a dramatic appearance by Pope John Paul II at Auschwitz. He paid tribute June 7, 1979, to the millions killed at the camps and made special reference to the Jewish martyrs, citing also Father Maximilian Kolbe, Edith Stein and others. In this homily the pope awakens the remembrance of millions of victims of the tragic slaughter. (Oswiecim was known during World War II by its German name Auschwitz.)

I have come and I kneel on this Golgotha of the modern world, on these tombs, largely nameless like the great Tomb of the Unknown Soldier. I kneel before all the inscriptions that come one after another bearing the memory of the victims of Oswiecim in the languages: Polish, English, Bulgarian, Romany, Czech, Danish, French, Greek, Hebrew, Yiddish, Spanish, Flemish, Serbo-Croat, German, Norwegian, Russian, Romanian, Hungarian and Italian.

In particular I pause with you, dear participants in this encounter, before the inscription in Hebrew. This inscription awakens the memory of the people whose sons and daughters were intended for total extermination. This people draws its origin from Abraham, our father in faith (cf. Rom 4:12), as was expressed by Paul of Tarsus. The very people who received from God the commandment "thou shalt not kill" itself experienced in a special measure what is meant by killing. It is not permissible for anyone to pass by this inscription with indifference.

To the Jewish Community—Battery Park

October 3, 1979

When Pope John Paul II revisited New York's Battery Park on October 3, 1979, he commented that the Jewish and Christian communities were closely related at the level of their respective religious identities, which can be the source of fraternal dialogue and fruitful collaboration.

I address a special word of greeting to the leaders of the Jewish community whose presence here honors me greatly. A few months ago, I met with an international group of Jewish representatives in Rome. On that occasion, recalling the initiatives undertaken following the Second Vatican Council under my predecessor, Paul VI, I stated that "our two communities are connected and closely related at the very level of their respective religious identities," and that on this basis "we recognize with utmost clarity that the path along which we should proceed is one of fraternal dialogue and fruitful collaboration" (*L'Osservatore Romano,* March 12–13, 1979). I am glad to ascertain that this same path has been followed here, in the United States, by large sections of both communities and their respective authorities and representative bodies. Several common programs of study, mutual knowledge, a common determination to reject all forms of antisemitism and discrimination, and various forms of collaboration for human advancement, inspired by our common biblical heritage, have created deep and permanent links between Jews and Catholics. As one who in my homeland has shared the suffering of your brethren, I greet you with the word taken from the Hebrew language: Shalom! Peace be with you.

27

1980

To a Group from the British Council of Christians and Jews at General Audience

March 19, 1980

I am pleased to offer a special word of greeting to members of the Council of Christians and Jews coming from various parts of the British Isles. I am aware that the purpose of your association is to strive to overcome prejudice, intolerance and discrimination, and to work for the betterment of human relations. I wish to express my cordial encouragement of your praiseworthy aims, and I gladly invoke upon all of you abundant divine blessings.

Meeting with Jews in Paris

May 31, 1980

While in France the pope met with representatives of the Jewish community on May 31, 1980. He paid tribute to the pioneers like Jules Isaac who opened the way to the present active stage of dialogue and collaboration between the church and Judaism. He called for a deepening of these relationships so that, united by the biblical ideal, Jews and Christians might work together for a society free of discrimination and a world at peace.

Dear Brothers,

It is a joy for me to receive the representatives of the numerous and vigorous Jewish community of France. This community has, indeed, a long and glorious history. It is necessary to recall here the theologians, exegetes, philosophers, and personages of public life who have distinguished it in the past and still distinguish it. It is true also, and I make a point of mentioning it, that your community suffered a great deal during the dark years of the occupation and the war. I pay homage to these victims, whose sacrifice, we know, has not been

29

fruitless. It was from there that there really began, thanks to the courage and decision of some pioneers, including Jules Isaac, the movement that has led us to the present dialogue and collaboration, inspired and promoted by the declaration *Nostra Aetate* of the Second Vatican Council.

This dialogue and this collaboration are very much alive and active here in France. This makes me happy. Between Judaism and the church, there is a relationship, as I said on another occasion to Jewish representatives, a relationship "at the very level of their respective religious identities" (*Address* of March 12, 1979). This relationship must be further deepened and enriched by study, mutual knowledge, religious education on both sides, and the effort to overcome the difficulties that still exist. That will enable us to work together for a society free of discriminations and prejudices, in which love and not hatred, peace and not war, justice and not oppression, may reign. It is towards this biblical ideal that we should always look, since it unites us so deeply. I take advantage of this happy opportunity to reaffirm it to you again and to express to you my hope of pursuing it together.

Remarks to the Jewish Community in Sao Paulo

July 3, 1980

On July 3, 1980, representatives of the Jewish community in Sao Paulo, Brazil heard Pope John Paul adverting to the religious frictions of the past but stressing the interfaith cooperation, especially of Jewish–Christian leadership and the present-day friendships as well as the bonds that unite the church with the descendants of Abraham in Brazil.

I am very happy to be able to greet you, the representatives of the Jewish community of Brazil, which is so vibrant and active in Sao Paulo, in Rio de Janeiro and in other cities. And I thank you from the bottom of my heart for your great friendliness in wanting to meet with me on the occasion of this apostolic journey to the great Brazilian nation. For me, it is a happy opportunity to show and to tighten the bonds that link the Catholic Church and Judaism here in Brazil, and reaffirm in this way the importance of the relations that are developing between us.

As you know, the Declaration *Nostra Aetate* of the Second Vatican Council, in its fourth paragraph, affirms that in scrutinizing its own mystery the church "remembers the bond that unites it with the descendants of Abraham." In this way the relation between the church and Judaism is not external to the two religions: it is something that is based on the distinctive religious heritage of both, on the very origins of Jesus and the apostles and in the environment within which the early church grew and developed.

In spite of this, our respective religious identities have divided us, at times grievously, through the centuries. This should not be an obstacle to our now respecting this same identity, wanting to emphasize our common heritage and in this way to cooperate, in light of this same heritage, for the solution of problems which afflict contemporary society, a society needing faith in God, obedience to his holy laws, active hope in the coming of his kingdom.

I am very pleased to know that this relationship of cooperation already exists here in Brazil, especially through the Judeo-Christian brotherhood. Thus Jews and Catholics strive to deepen the common biblical heritage without, however, trying to conceal the differences which separate us and in this way a renewed mutual knowledge can lead to a more adequate presentation of each religion in the teaching of the other. Upon this solid base, cooperation for the benefit of concrete man, promotion of his rights, not rarely trod upon, of his just participation in the pursuit of the common good, without exclusiveness or discrimination, can be built up, as it is now being built.

These, moreover, are some of the points brought to the attention of the Catholic community by the *Orientations and Suggestions for the Application of the Council Declaration Nostra Aetate* published by the Commission for Religious Relations with Judaism in 1975, as well as by the corresponding paragraphs of the final document of the Conference of Puebla (n. 1110, 1123).

This will make the valuable spiritual patrimony that joins Jews and Christians vibrant and effective for the good of all. This I desire with all my heart. And this will hopefully be the fruit of this brotherly encounter with the representatives of the Jewish community of Brazil.

Homily at Otranto, Italy

October 5, 1980

On Sunday, October 5, 1980 the Holy Father concluded his pilgrimage to Otranto with the celebration of Mass on the Hill of the Martyrs, commemorating the 500th anniversary of the death of Blessed Antonio

31

Primoldo and his 800 companions. The pope delivered the following homily.

Prayer for Middle East

At the same time we cannot close our eyes to particularly delicate situations that have developed there and still exist. Harsh conflicts have broken out; the Middle East region is pervaded by tensions and strife, with the ever incumbent risk of the outbreak of new wars. It is painful to note that conflicts have often taken place following the lines of division between different confessional groups, so that it has been possible for some people, unfortunately, to feed them artificially by appealing to the religious sentiment.

The terms of the Middle East drama are well known: the Jewish People, after tragic experiences connected with the extermination of so many sons and daughters, driven by the desire for security, set up the State of Israel. At the same time the painful condition of the Palestinian People was created, a large part of whom are excluded from their land. These are facts that are before everyone's eyes. And other countries, such as Lebanon, are suffering as a result of a crisis which threatens to be a chronic one. In these days, finally, a bitter conflict is in progress in a neighbouring region, between Irak and Iran.

Gathered here today, at the tombs of the Martyrs of Otranto, let us meditate on the words of the liturgy, which proclaim their glory and their power in the Kingdom of God: "They will govern nations and rule over peoples, and the Lord will reign over them for ever". Therefore in union with these Martyrs, we present to the One God, to the Living God, to the Father of all men, the problems of peace in the Middle East and also the problem, which is so dear to us, of the rapport and real dialogue with those with whom we are united—in spite of the differences—by faith in one God, the faith inherited from Abraham. May the spirit of unity, mutual respect and understanding prove to be more powerful than what divides and sets in opposition.

Lebanon, Palestine, Egypt, the Arabian Peninsula, Mesopotamia nourished for millennia the roots of traditions sacred for each of the three religious groups. There again, for centuries, Christian, Jewish, and Islamic communities lived together on the same territories; in those regions, the Catholic Church boasts communities outstanding for their ancient history, vitality, variety of rites, and their own spiritual characteristics.

Towering high over all this world, like an ideal centre, a precious jewel-case that keeps the treasures of the most venerable memories, and is itself the first of these treasures, is the Holy City, Jerusalem, today the object of a dispute that seems without a solution, tomorrow—if people only want it!—tomorrow a crossroads of reconciliation and peace.

Yes, we pray that Jerusalem, instead of being as it is today the object of strife and division, may become the meeting point towards which the eyes of Christians, Jews, and Moslems will continue to turn, as to their own common hearth; round which they will feel as brothers, no one superior, no one in the debt of others; towards which pilgrims, followers of Christ, or faithful of Mosaic law, or members of the community of Islam, will continue to direct their steps.

Address to the Jewish Community—W. Germany

November 17, 1980

Pope John Paul spoke to representatives of the Jewish community November 17, 1980, at Mainz, West Germany. He pointed out that an address such as this is not merely a matter of correcting a false religious view of the Jewish people but is above all, "a question of the dialogue between the two religions which with Islam can give to the world the belief in one ineffable God who speaks to us and which, representing the entire world, wish to serve him."

Shalom!

Ladies and Gentlemen, Dear Brothers and Sisters!

I thank you for your friendly and sincere words of greeting. This meeting was a deep need for me in the framework of this apostolic journey, and I thank you for fulfilling it. May God's blessing accompany this hour!

1. If Christians must consider themselves brothers of all men and behave accordingly, this holy obligation is all the more binding when they find themselves before members of the Jewish people! In the "Declaration on the relationship of the Church with Judaism" in April of this year, the Bishops of the Federal Republic of Germany put this sentence at the beginning: "Whoever meets Jesus Christ, meets Ju-

daism". I would like to make these words mine too. The faith of the Church in Jesus Christ, the son of David and the son of Abraham (cf. Mt 1:1) actually contains what the bishops call in that declaration "the spiritual heritage of Israel for the Church" (par. 11), a living heritage, which must be understood and preserved in its depth and richness by us Catholic Christians.

2. The concrete brotherly relations between Jews and Catholics in Germany assume a quite particular value against the grim background of the persecution and the attempted extermination of Judaism in this country. The innocent victims in Germany and elsewhere, the families destroyed or dispersed, the cultural values or art treasures destroyed forever, are a tragic proof where discrimination and contempt of human dignity can lead, especially if they are animated by perverse theories on a presumed difference in the value of races or on the division of men into men of "high worth", "worthy of living", and men who are "worthless", "unworthy of living". Before God all men are of the same value and importance.

In this spirit, during the persecution, Christians likewise committed themselves, often at the risk of their lives, to prevent or relieve the sufferings of their Jewish brothers and sisters. I would like to express recognition and gratitude to them at this moment. And also to those people who, as Christians, affirming they belonged to the Jewish people, travelled along the *via crucis* of their brothers and sisters to the end—like the great Edith Stein, called in her religious institute Teresa Benedikta of the Cross, whose memory is rightly held in great honour.

I would further like to mention also Franz Rosenzweig and Martin Buber, who, through their creative familiarity with the Jewish and German languages, constructed a wonderful bridge for a deeper meeting of both cultural areas.

You yourselves stressed, in your words of greeting, that in the many efforts to build up a new common life with Jewish citizens in this country, Catholics and the Church have made a decisive contribution. This recognition and the necessary collaboration on your part fills me with joy. For my part, I wish to express grateful admiration also for your initiatives in this connection, including the recent foundation of your Heidelberg University.

3. The depth and richness of our common heritage are revealed to us particularly in friendly dialogue and trusting collaboration. I rejoice that, in this country, conscious and zealous care is dedicated to all this. Many public and private initiatives in the pastoral, academic, and social field serve this purpose, as on very solemn occasions

such as the recent one at the Katholikentag in Berlin. Also an encouraging sign was the meeting of the international liaison committee between the Roman Catholic Church and Judaism in Regensburg last year.

It is not just a question of correcting a false religious view of the Jewish people, which in the course of history was one of the causes that contributed to misunderstanding and persecution, but above all of the dialogue between the two religions which—with Islam—gave the world faith in the one, ineffable God who speaks to us, and which desire to serve him on behalf of the whole world.

The first dimension of this dialogue, that is, the meeting between the people of God of the Old Covenant, never revoked by God (cf. Rom 11:29), and that of the New Covenant, is at the same time a dialogue within our Church, that is to say, between the first and the second part of her Bible. In this connection the directives for the application of the conciliar Declaration *Nostra Aetate* say: "The effort must be made to understand better everything in the Old Testament that has its own, permanent value . . ., since this value is not wiped out by the later interpretation of the New Testament, which, on the contrary, gave the Old Testament its full meaning, so that it is a question rather of reciprocal enlightenment and explanation" (n. 11).

A second dimension of our dialogue—the true and central one—is the meeting between the present-day Christian Churches and the present-day people of the covenant concluded with Moses. It is important here "that Christians—so continue the post-conciliar directives—should aim at understanding better the fundamental elements of the religious tradition of Judaism, and learn what fundamental lines are essential for the religious reality lived by the Jews, according to their own understanding" (Introduction). The way for this mutual knowledge is dialogue. I thank you, venerated brothers and sisters, for carrying it out, you too, with that "openness and breadth of spirit", with that "tact" and with that "prudence" which are recommended to us Catholics by the above-mentioned directives. A fruit of this dialogue and an indication for its fruitful continuation, is the declaration of German bishops quoted at the beginning "on the relationship between the Church and Judaism" in April of this year. It is my eager desire that this declaration should become the spiritual property of all Catholics in Germany!

I would also like to refer briefly to a third dimension of our dialogue. The German bishops dedicate the concluding chapter of their declaration to the tasks which we have in common. Jews and Christians, as children of Abraham, are called to be a blessing for the world (cf.

Gn 12:2ff.), by committing themselves together for peace and justice among all men and peoples, with the fullness and depth that God himself intended us to have, and with the readiness for sacrifices that this high goal may demand. The more our meeting is imprinted with this sacred duty, the more it becomes a blessing also for ourselves.

4. In the light of this promise and call of Abraham's, I look with you to the destiny and role of your people among the peoples. I willingly pray with you for the fullness of Shalom for all your brothers, in nationality and in faith, and also for the land to which Jews look with particular veneration. Our century saw the first pilgrimage of a Pope to the Holy Land. In conclusion, I wish to repeat Paul VI's words on entering Jerusalem: "Implore with us, in your desire and in your prayer, respect and peace upon this unique land, visited by God! Let us pray here together for the grace of a real and deep brotherhood between all men, between all peoples! . . . May they who love you be blessed. Yes, may peace dwell in your walls, prosperity in your palaces. I pray for peace for you. I desire happiness for you" (cf. Ps 122:6-9).

May all peoples in Jerusalem soon be reconciled and blessed in Abraham! May he, the ineffable, of whom his creation speaks to us: he, who does not force mankind to goodness, but guides it: he, who manifests himself in our fate and is silent; he, who chooses all of us as his people; may he guide us along his ways to his future!

Praised be his Name! Amen.

1982

To Delegates to the Meeting of Representatives of Episcopal Conferences and Other Experts in Catholic-Jewish Relations: Commission for Religious Relations with Judaism

March 6, 1982

Dear Brothers in the Episcopate and in the Priesthood, Sisters, Ladies and Gentlemen:

From different parts of the world we are here assembled in Rome to see where we stand regarding the important question of relations between the Catholic Church and Judaism. And the importance of this problem is also underlined by the presence among you of representatives of the Orthodox Churches, of the Anglican Communion, of the Lutheran World Federation and the World Council of Churches, whom I am particularly happy to greet and to thank for their collaboration.

I express equally my gratitude to all of you who are here, bishops, priests, religious and lay men and women. Your presence here, just as your involvement in pastoral activities or in the domain of biblical and theological research, reveals to what extent the relations between the Catholic Church and Judaism touch on different aspects of the life and activities of the Church.

And this, one can easily understand. The Second Vatican Council said in effect in its declaration on the relations between the Church and the non-Christian religions (*Nostra Aetate,* n. 4): "As this Sacred Synod searches into the mystery of the Church, it recalls the spiritual bond linking the people of the New Covenant with Abraham's stock". And I myself have had an opportunity to say so on more than one occasion: "our two religious communities are connected and closely related at the very level of their religious identities" (cf. *Speech* of 12 March 1979, to the representatives of Jewish Organizations and Communities). Indeed, and it is again the very text of the Declaration

37

(*Nostra Aetate*, n. 4), "the Church of Christ acknowledges that, according to the mystery of God's saving design, the beginnings of her faith and her election are already found among the patriarchs, Moses and the Prophets. . . . The Church, therefore, cannot forget that she received the revelation of the Old Testament through this people. . . . Also the Church ever keeps in mind the words of the Apostle about his kinsmen 'who have the adoption as sons, and the glory and the covenants and the legislation and the worship and the promises, who have the fathers, and from whom is Christ according to the flesh' (Rom 9:4-5), the son of the Virgin Mary".

This means that the links between the Church and the Jewish people are founded on the design of the God of the Covenant and—as such—have necessarily left their traces in certain aspects of the institutions of the Church, particularly in her liturgy.

Certainly, since the appearance, two thousand years ago, of a new branch from the common root, relations between our two communities have been marked by the misunderstandings and resentments with which we are familiar. And if, since the day of the separation, there have been misunderstandings, errors, indeed offences, it is now our task to leave these behind with understanding, peace and mutual respect. The terrible persecutions suffered by the Jews in different periods of history have finally opened the eyes of many and appalled many people's hearts. Christians have taken the right path, that of justice and brotherhood, in seeking to come together with their Semitic brethren, respectfully and perseveringly, in the common heritage, a heritage that all value so highly. Should it not be pointed out, especially to those who remain sceptical, even hostile, that this reconciliation should not be confused with a sort of religious relativism, less still with a loss of identity? Christians, for their part, profess their faith unequivocally in the universal salvific significance of the death and resurrection of Jesus of Nazareth.

Yes, the clarity and affirmation of our Christian identity constitute an essential basis if we are to have real, productive and durable ties with the Jewish people. In this sense I am happy to know that you dedicate much effort in study and prayer together, the better to grasp and formulate the sometimes complex biblical and theological problems which have arisen because of the very progress of Judaeo-Christian dialogue. Work that is of poor quality or lacking in precision would be extremely detrimental to dialogue in this field. May God allow Christians and Jews really to come together, to arrive at an exchange in depth, founded on their respective identities, but never blurring it on either side, truly searching the will of God the Revealer.

Such relations can and should contribute to a richer knowledge of our own roots, and will certainly cast light on some aspects of the Christian identity just mentioned. Our common spiritual patrimony is very large.

To assess it carefully in itself and with due awareness of the faith and religious life of the Jewish people as they are professed and practised still today, can greatly help us to understand better certain aspects of the life of the Church. Such is the case of liturgy whose Jewish roots remain still to be examined in depth, and in any case should be better known and appreciated by our faithful. The same is true of the history of our institutions which, since the beginning of the Church, have been inspired by certain aspects of the synagogue community organization. Finally our common spiritual patrimony is particularly important when we turn to our belief in one only God, good and merciful, who loves men and is loved by them (cf. Wis 24:26), Lord of history and of the destinies of men, who is our Father and who chose Israel, "the good olive tree onto which have been grafted the wild olive branches, that of the gentiles" (*Nostra Aetate,* n. 4; cf. also Rom 11:17-24).

This is why you yourselves were concerned, during your sessions, with Catholic teaching and catechesis regarding Jews and Judaism. On this particular point, as on many others, you have been guided and encouraged by the "Orientations and Suggestions for the Application of the Conciliar Declaration *'Nostra Aetate'* n. 4", published by the Commission for religious relations with Judaism (see chapter 3). We should aim, in this field, that Catholic teaching at its different levels, in catechesis to children and young people, presents Jews and Judaism, not only in an honest and objective manner, free from prejudices and without any offences, but also with full awareness of the heritage we have sketched above.

It is ultimately on such a basis that it will be possible to establish—as we know is happily already the case—a close collaboration towards which our common heritage directs us, in service of man and his vast spiritual and material needs. Through different but finally convergent ways we will be able to reach, with the help of the Lord who has never ceased to love his people (cf. Rom 11:1), this true brotherhood in reconciliation and respect and to contribute to a full implementation of God's plan in history.

I am happy to encourage you, dear brothers and sisters in Christ, to continue on the path that has been begun, using discernment and trust and at the same time with great faithfulness to the Church's Magisterium. In such way you will render the Church a great service which flows from her mysterious vocation. This should contribute to the good of the Church itself, of the Jewish people and of the whole of humanity.

To Religious Leaders in Portugal

Lisbon

May 14, 1982

During his 1982 visit to Portugal, the Pope gave new proofs of his respect for non-Christian religious traditions. On May 14, at Lisbon, speaking to a group of Jews, Christians, and Moslems, he affirmed:

Abraham, our common ancestor, teaches all of us, Christians, Jews, and Moslems, to follow this way of mercy and love.

Sameiro

May 15, 1982

Then, on May 15, at Sameiro in the Archdiocese of Braga, the Pope spoke of Jesus:

Born during the night at Bethlehem, the son of Mary thus entered into the spiritual inheritance of Israel—of his people.

The text of the Pope's May 14 address to Jewish, Christian, and Moslem representatives in Lisbon follows:

Gentlemen and my Brothers,

1. I am grateful for the respectful words and for the good wishes that have been addressed to me, and I wish to greet the representatives of the Christian, the Jewish, and the Islamic communities here present, expressing to all of them fraternal respect and esteem. To be able to affirm today, together, faith in one God, creator of all things, living, almighty and merciful, would be enough in itself to make this meeting a pleasure for me; I am happy that this opportunity to bear witness, which is at the same time homage and an act of submission to our God, has been offered to us.

We are united in some way by faith and by a commitment, similar in many ways, to demonstrate by good works the consistency of our respective religious positions; and also the desire that, honouring as Lord the Creator of all things, our example may serve to help others in the search for God, in the opening toward transcendence, in recognition of the spiritual value of the human person and, at times, in the identification of the foundation and permanent source of man's rights. This—we well know—is the condition in which criteria of esteem for the human being may exist, which are not limited to "practical usefulness", but which may safeguard his intangible dignity. In addition to this, as far as Christians are concerned, common faith in Christ the Saviour is a special reason for unity and witness.

2. Contemporary society seems to us to be heedless of, or even inclined on a wide scale to "prescind" from, God and religion, and to be greatly absorbed in the earthly and material dimensions of man and life: admirable progress in all fields secure great benefits, but they seem to encourage in some people a reversal and substitution of values. By recognizing and proclaiming spiritual and religious values, we can certainly bring about and guide a general vital insight and, among persons in normal situations, a certain conceptual glimmer of the reality of a subsisting Creator.

On the other hand, there is always room for human solidarity in the fidelity to the religion we embrace since, convinced as we are of the good which belief in God constitutes for us, the desire to share this good with others is spontaneous. In all respect, we can make ourselves a symbol of the Almighty: he who for many is the "unknown God"; for others, he is erroneously symbolized by temporal powers, inexorably marked by their transience and frailness.

3. Our contacts, dialogue and appreciation for the undeniable treasures of every religion's spirituality, Christian community and, when it is possible, common prayer, can lead to the convergence of efforts to avert the illusion of building a new world without God, and the vanity of a purely anthropocentric humanism. Without the religious dimension and, even worse, without religious freedom, man is impoverished or cheated of one of his basic rights. And we all wish to avoid this impoverishment of man.

So, when motivated also by human solidarity, we pass from prayer, from obedience to the commandments and from the observance of justice to concretely living our religious adherence aiding the search for God, we are contributing to the good of our neighbour and to the common good of humanity. And this can be verified:

—through personal honesty and discipline of habits in private and

41

public life, halting the advance of the slackening of moral principles and those of justice, as well as ethical permissiveness;

—in respect for life and for the family and its values, fostering the uplifting, in humanity and dignity, of our fellow men and the consolidation of the irreplaceable bases for harmonious living together in society;

—by reverence for the authentic meaning and generous practice of human work, and with courageous and knowledgeable social and political participation, seeking the well-being of everyone and the building of societies and the world, always more in accord with the plans and decrees of God, throughout the world, since only in this way can there be a more just, peaceful world imbued with brotherly love.

4. As you know, I have come to Portugal in pilgrimage, primarily to celebrate God's mercy. Within me is the deep conviction that the merciful God wishes to see this characteristic more clearly reflected in the entire human family: authentic mercy seems to me something which is indispensable to giving shape and solidity to relations among men, inspired by the deepest respect for all that is human and for brotherhood.

In effect, Christians are exhorted to imitate the Lord Jesus, model of mercy. Judaism also considers mercy a fundamental commandment. And Islamism, in its profession of faith, attributes this trait to God. And Abraham, our common ancestor, teaches everyone—Christians, Jews and Muslims—to follow this way of mercy and of love.

May I be allowed to conclude my remarks by lifting up my spirit in a prayer to the merciful God:

—O Ineffable One, of whom all creation speaks,

—O Almighty One, who never forces, but only invites and guides mankind toward good,

—O Compassionate One, who desires mercy among all men: may he always guide us along his paths, fill our hearts with his love, with his peace and joy, and bless us!

Visit to Great Britain

Manchester

May 31, 1982

On the occasion of his 1982 visit to Great Britain, the Pope twice met with leaders of the Jewish Community. On May 31, during his visit to Manchester, Pope John Paul II was welcomed by the Vice-President

of the Jewish Board of Deputies of Britain, Lionel Kopelowitz, who spoke to him in Polish. Following an address by the Chief Rabbi of Great Britain, Sir Emmanuel Jakobovits, the Pope replied ex tempore.

The Chief Rabbi's speech, although very brief, was most comprehensive in the way in which it looked realistically both at the various aspects of the unhappy past of Jewish-Christian relations and also at the warmth of the present situation from the time of Pope John XXIII.

The Chief Rabbi, Sir Emmanuel Jakobovits, welcomed the Pope:

The Pope's visit to this country, although officially of a pastoral nature, is an historical event of significance far beyond Catholic friends. British Jews join their fellow citizens in warmly greeting you not only as the world's most widely acclaimed spiritual leader, but as a charismatic personality of rare distinction, deeply respected for his vision, dynamic qualities and human virtues.

These ecumenical aspirations, while primarily of inter-Christian concern, are of course of profound interest to Jews as well, much more so since the papacy had often been a cause of conflict and suffering in the long history of the Jewish people and happily, past tragic relations have lately been reversed, notably by the enlightened policies of Catholic-Jewish reconciliation pioneered by Pope John XXIII, a momentous turning point to which the late Cardinal Heenan gave such powerful momentum.

As Pope John Paul II, you have maintained and further promoted this inter-faith understanding, yourself hailing from a country in which you witnessed and shared the supreme agony of the Nazi holocaust, including the massacre of three million Polish Jews.

Your election aroused special interest among the Jewish people. Also of particular relevance to Jews are the as yet unpredictable consequences of the religious stirring within the communist world sparked by the Catholic revival in Poland under your spell.

These consequences may well eventually alleviate the bonds of more than three million Soviet Jews among the repressed religious communities. In the USSR and her satellite countries, as senior progenitors of the Judaeo-Christian heritage which nurtured Western civilizations, the Jewish people watched with profound gratification your immense efforts to reassert the moral and spiritual values we have in common against the disruptive inroads of violence, the blighting depression of materialism, and the de-spiritualized secularization which threatens everything we have built up over the ages and may even endanger human survival itself.

Whilst enormous strides had been made in defending Jewish-Christian harmony, some items on our common agenda still remain to be

43

resolved. They include the elimination of the last vestiges of religious prejudices against Jews and some residual Christian hesitations in accepting the State of Israel as the fulfilment of millennial Jewish dreams.

We seek understanding for our love of Jerusalem, a city holy to three faiths because Jews first sanctified it as their capital 5,000 years ago.

This anxious time, when our country is sadly once again at war with significant loss of life in defence of freedom and the rule of law, we pray with special fervour that your visit may contribute to the advancement of reconciliation and peace, inspiration and the blessing of rededication to the noblest ideas of human brotherhood.

The Holy Father replied:

I should first say that I followed your speech with great interest and I pondered the agruments you included in this speech. My answer is rather brief and not so full of arguments as your speech, but I am very grateful for your having put all these questions in your speech.

It is a joy for me to extend my fraternal greetings this morning to you, leading members of the Jewish Community. Particularly I greet the Chief Rabbi of the Commonwealth, Sir Emmanuel Jakobovits, together with other distinguished colleagues. On the occasion of my visit to Britain I wish to express my personal sentiments of esteem and friendship for all of you. At the same time I wish to reiterate the full respect of the Catholic Church for the Jewish people throughout the world. In the spirit of the Second Vatican Council, I recall the desire of the Church to collaborate willingly with you in the great cause of mankind, knowing that we have a common tradition that honours the sanctity of God and calls us to love the Lord our God with all our heart and with all our soul.

I extend cordial greetings to all those whom you represent.

Scotland

June 1, 1982

And on the following day in Scotland, during the course of a meeting with various religious leaders, the Pope included the following reference to its Jewish community:

I am happy to greet also the representatives of the Jewish community in Scotland, who, through their presence here, symbolize the profound spiritual links which unite our two religious communities so closely together.

To Leaders of the Jewish Community, Madrid

November 3, 1982

Gentlemen,

Shalom! Peace be to you and all the members of the Jewish religious community in Spain.

First of all, I want to tell you how much I appreciate your readiness to come to meet me during my pastoral visit to this country. This significant gesture of yours is a proof that the fraternal dialogue, which seeks to improve knowledge and mutual esteem between Jews and Catholics and which was promoted and warmly recommended by the Second Vatican Council in its Declaration *Nostra Aetate* (n. 4), is continuing and becoming more widespread, notwithstanding inevitable difficulties.

We have a common spiritual heritage; the People of the New Testament, that is to say the Church, feels itself and is spiritually bound to the stock of Abraham, "our father in the faith".

I pray to God that the Jewish and Christian tradition, founded on the Word of God, which has so profound an awareness of the dignity of the human person made in the image of God (cf. Gn 1:26), will lead us to fervent worship and love of the one true God; and that this will be translated into effective action on behalf of men, each man and every man.

Shalom! May God, the Creator and Saviour, bless you and your community.

1983

On the Fortieth Anniversary of the Warsaw Ghetto Uprising

April 13 and 25, 1983

On April 25, 1983 the Pope received in audience a Jewish delegation from the Simon Wiesenthal Center, Los Angeles, returning from the ceremonies which commemorated the fortieth anniversary of the Warsaw Ghetto Uprising in Poland. The following is the text of the Pontiff's address on that occasion:

Dear Friends,

I extend a warm greeting to all the members of the delegation organized by the Simon Wiesenthal Center of Los Angeles. I am very pleased to welcome you to the Vatican today and in this way to further the continuing religious dialogue between Judaism and the Catholic Church. Such meetings as ours deepen bonds of friendship and trust and help us to appreciate more fully the richness of our common heritage as people who believe in the one Lord and God who has revealed himself to man.

As Christians and Jews, as children of Abraham, we are called to be a blessing for the world (cf. Gn 12:2ff) especially by our witness in faith to God, the source of all life, and by our commitment to work together for the establishment of true peace and justice among all peoples and nations. Taking up the way of dialogue and mutual collaboration, we deepen bonds of friendship and trust among ourselves and offer to others a sign of hope for the future.

I am happy to know that your itinerary has included a visit to Poland to commemorate the Fortieth Anniversary of the Warsaw ghetto uprising. Just recently, speaking of that horrible and tragic event of history, I said: "It was a desperate cry for the right of life, for liberty and for the salvation of human dignity. . . . Paying homage to the memory of these innocent victims, we pray: may the Eternal God accept this sacrifice for the well-being and the salvation of the world."

May God bless you and your families with harmony and peace. May he bless you with the fullness of Shalom.

Some days previously, on April 13, at his general audience, the Pope made allusion to his pilgrimage to Auschwitz in 1979 in the following terms:

During my pilgrimage to Auschwitz in June 1979, standing before the stone engraved in Hebrew characters which is dedicated to the victims of this death camp, I spoke the following words:

> This inscription calls to mind that people whose sons and daughters were destined for total extermination. This people traces its beginnings back to Abraham, the father of our faith (cf. Rom 4:12) as expressed by Paul of Tarsus. This same people, which had received from God the commandment: "Thou shalt not kill" has felt in itself in a special way what it means to be killed. No one, passing in front of this stone, can remain indifferent to its message.

Today I want to recall those words to mind again, remembering with all the Church in Poland and the whole Jewish people the terrible days of the uprising and of the destruction of the Warsaw Ghetto forty years ago (from April 19 to the middle of July, 1943). It was a desperate cry for the right to life, for liberty and for the salvation of human dignity. . . .

To the Catholics of France, Lourdes

August 15, 1983

The Pope does not always reserve his comments on Catholic-Jewish relations just for official meetings with Jewish delegations. Often, as in this excerpt from a major address to French Catholics in Lourdes, he will remind the Catholic community of its responsibility for dialogue. The present excerpt stands for many similar ones that might have been chosen.

IV. And now, I give my cordial greeting and good wishes to these who, *without being Catholic,* share the *Christian faith.* With you we desire to correspond better to the will of Christ and actively to pursue the road to unity. I am sure also that faith in the one God can be a powerful leaven of harmony and collaboration among Christians, *Jews and Muslims* in the struggle against the prejudices and suspicions that ought to be overcome.

In the same spirit of respect and friendship, I do not hesitate to address the inhabitants of this country who are *non-believers,* or who are troubled by doubt regarding the faith. We often have in common a loyal dedication to the same humanitarian causes, the concern for justice, fellowship, peace, respect for human dignity, and help to the most disadvantaged. I extend my best wishes to you and to your families.

For all of them as well as for the believers, I wish to add this. In tenaciously acting throughout the world for the respect of religious liberty, the Church of today is clearly aware of taking the lead in a necessary combat for the human person, for the most basic human liberty, for the defence of all the other basic liberties. I know that this land of France is singularly committed to such a struggle for liberty and human dignity. The Church is convinced—and the example of the saints I just recalled demonstrates it—that the spark of faith and sanctity can grow only in a free heart. The Church, therefore, is more attentive than others to the respect that every honest step towards this end deserves.

"Europe Vespers," Vienna

September 10, 1983

A highlight of the Pope's 1983 trip to Austria was the celebration of the "Europe Vespers," reflecting Vienna's unique role as a crossroad between East and West. The Pope reflected on the historic role of the city in both Christian-Jewish and Christian-Muslim relations. In the seventeenth century the city successfully resisted the last great Muslim invasion of Europe, marking the end of an era. In a different and tragic way, the destruction of the Jewish community of Vienna symbolizes the end of another era in European history:

3. ... The history of Europe is marked by discord not only in the sphere of states and politics. *Schisms* have divided also the one Church of Jesus Christ. In conjunction with political interests and social problems, these have resulted in bitter fighting, in the oppression and expulsion of dissenters, in repression and intolerance. As heirs to our

forebears, we also place this guilt-ridden Europe under the Cross. For in the Cross is our hope.

5. . . . A special legacy of the decisive events of 1683 to the Christian Churches is above all the cause of religious peace—peace between the heirs of Abraham and unity among the brothers of Jesus Christ. The disciples of Mahomet, who then besieged your capital city, now live in your midst and many of them may serve as a model for us in their devout worship of the one God. The fate of the Jewish community, once so fruitfully integrated into the nations of Europe, now so tragically decimated, admonishes us to seize every opportunity for promoting human and spiritual understanding, so that we can stand before God together, and to serve humanity in his spirit. The rift among Christians, so fateful in its impact in 1683 also on the political level, now constitutes an opportunity, even a challenge, to move forward towards a community united in prayer and charitable service.

1984

To Anti-Defamation League of B'nai B'rith

March 22, 1984

Dear Friends,

I am very happy to receive you here in the Vatican. You are a group of national and international leaders of the well-known Jewish Association, based in the United States, but active in many parts of the world, including Rome itself, the Anti-Defamation League of B'nai B'rith. You are also closely related with the Commission for Religious Relations with Judaism, founded ten years ago by Paul VI for the purpose of fostering relations, at the level of our respective faith commitment, between the Catholic Church and the Jewish Community.

The mere fact of your visit to me, for which I am grateful, is in itself a proof of the constant development and deepening of such relations. Indeed, when one looks back to the years before the Second Vatican Council and its Declaration *Nostra Aetate* and tries to encompass the work done since, one has the feeling that the Lord has done "great things" for us (cf. Lk 1:49). Therefore we are called to join in a heartfelt act of thanksgiving to God. The opening verse of Psalm 133 is appropriate: "How good and pleasant it is when brothers dwell in unity".

Because, my dear friends, as I have often said since the beginning of my pastoral service as Successor of Peter, the Galilean fisherman (cf. allocution of 12 March 1979), the encounter between Catholics and Jews is not a meeting of two ancient religions each going its own way, and not infrequently, in times past, in grievous and painful conflict. It is a meeting between "brothers", a dialogue, as I said to the Representatives of the German Jewish community in Mainz (17 November 1980), "between the first and the second part of the Bible". And as the two parts of the Bible are distinct but closely related, so are the Jewish people and the Catholic Church.

This closeness is to be manifested in many ways. First of all, in the deep respect for each other's identity. The more we know each other, the more we learn to assess and respect our differences.

51

But then, and this is the great challenge we are called to accept: respect does not mean estrangement, nor is it tantamount to indifference. On the contrary, the respect we speak of is based on the mysterious spiritual link (cf. *Nostra Aetate,* 4) which brings us close together, in Abraham and, through Abraham, in God who chose Israel and brought forth the Church from Israel.

This "spiritual link", however, involves a great responsibility. Closeness in respect implies trust and frankness, and totally excludes distrust and suspicion. It also calls for fraternal concern for one another and the problems and difficulties with which each of our religious communities is faced.

The Jewish community in general, and your organization in particular, as your name proclaims, are very much concerned with old and new forms of discrimination and violence against Jews and Judaism, ordinarily called anti-Semitism. The Catholic Church, even before the Second Vatican Council (cf. S. Congregation of the Holy Office, 3 March 1928; Pius XI to a group of Belgian radio-journalists, 6 September 1938) condemned such ideology and practice as opposed not only to the Christian profession but also to the dignity of the human person created in the image of God.

But we are not meeting each other just for ourselves. We certainly try to know each other better and to understand better our respective distinctive identity and the close spiritual link between us. But, knowing each other, we discover still more what brings us together for a deeper concern for humanity at large: in areas, to cite but a few, such as hunger, poverty, discrimination wherever it may be found and against whomever it may be directed, and the needs of refugees. And, certainly, the great task of promoting justice and peace (cf. Ps 85:4), the sign of the messianic age in both the Jewish and the Christian tradition, grounded in its turn in the great prophetic heritage. This "spiritual link" between us cannot fail to help us face the great challenge addressed to those who believe that God cares for all people, whom he created in his own image (cf. Gn 1:27).

I see this at the same time as a reality and as a promise of the dialogue between the Catholic Church and Judaism, and of the relations already existing between your organization and the Commission for Religious Relations with Judaism and with other institutions in some local Churches.

I thank you again for your visit and for your commitment to the goals of dialogue. Let us be grateful to our God, the Father of us all.

Apostolic Letter of John Paul II
Redemptionis Anno

April 20, 1984

To understand the Pope's message in this letter, one needs to understand it as a spiritual challenge, and not merely as a political statement. Likewise, one needs to read it within the context of the many statements on Christian-Jewish relations and the Middle East issued by the Holy See and bishops' conferences throughout the world since the promulgation almost two decades ago by the Second Vatican Council of the now famous declaration on the Jews, "Nostra Aetate", no. 4.

These statements, too numerous to be listed here, tell the story of a true "teshuvah," a turning on the part of Christianity regarding its understanding of Jews and Judaism, toward an understanding that acknowledges with respect and affirmation how the Jewish people views itself as a people. The letter, dated April 20, 1984 (Good Friday), follows:

Revered Brothers and beloved Sons,
   health and Apostolic Blessing.

As the Jubilee Year of Redemption draws to a close, my thoughts go to that special land which is located in that place where Europe, Asia and Africa meet and in which the Redemption of the human race was accomplished "once and for all" (Rom 6:10; Heb 7:27; 9:12; 10:10).

It is a land which we call holy, indeed the land which was the earthly homeland of Christ who walked about it "preaching the gospel of the kingdom and healing every disease and every infirmity" (Mt 4:23).

This year especially I was pleased to be touched by the same sentiment and the same joy as my predecessor Pope Paul VI, when he visited the Holy Land and Jerusalem in 1964.

Although I cannot be there physically, I nevertheless feel that I am spiritually a pilgrim in that land where our reconciliation with God was brought about, to beg the Prince of Peace for the gift of redemption and of peace which is so earnestly desired by the hearts of people, families, and nations—in a special way by the nations which inhabit this very area.

I think especially of the City of Jerusalem, where Jesus, offering his life "has made us both one, and has broken down the dividing wall of hostility . . . bringing the hostility to an end" (Eph 2:14, 16).

Before it was the city of Jesus the Redeemer, Jerusalem was the historic site of the biblical revelation of God, the meeting place, as it were, of heaven and earth, in which more than in any other place the word of God was brought to men.

Christians honour her with a religious and intent concern because there the words of Christ so often resounded, there the great events of the Redemption were accomplished: the Passion, Death and Resurrection of the Lord. In the City of Jerusalem the first Christian community sprang up and remained throughout the centuries a continual ecclesial presence despite difficulties.

Jews ardently love her and in every age venerate her memory, abundant as she is in many remains and monuments from the time of David who chose her as the capital, and of Solomon who built the Temple there. Therefore, they turn their minds to her daily, one may say, and point to her as the sign of their nation.

Muslims also call Jerusalem "Holy", with a profound attachment that goes back to the origins of Islam and springs from the fact that they have there many special places of pilgrimage and for more than a thousand years have dwelt there, almost without interruption.

Besides these exceptional and outstanding testimonies, Jerusalem contains communities of believers full of life, whose presence the peoples of the whole world regard as a sign and source of hope— especially those who consider the Holy City to be in a certain way their spiritual heritage and a symbol of peace and harmony.

Indeed, insofar as she is the homeland of the hearts of all the spiritual descendants of Abraham who hold her very dear, and the place where, according to faith, the created things of earth encounter the infinite transcendence of God, Jerusalem stands out as a symbol of coming together, of union, and of universal peace for the human family.

The Holy City, therefore, strongly urges peace for the whole human race, especially for those who worship the one, great God, the merciful Father of the peoples. But it must be acknowledged that Jerusalem continues to be the cause of daily conflict, violence and partisan reprisals.

This situation and these considerations cause these words of the Prophet to spring to the lips: "For Zion's sake I will not keep silent, and for Jerusalem's sake I will not rest, until her vindication goes forth as brightness, and her salvation as a burning torch" (Is 62:1).

I think of and long for the day on which we shall all be so "taught by God" (Jn 6:45) that we shall listen to his message of peace and reconciliation. I think of the day on which Jews, Christians and Muslims will greet each other in the city of Jerusalem with the same greeting of peace with which Christ greeted the disciples after the resurrection: "Peace be with you" (Jn 20:19).

The Roman Pontiffs, especially in this century, have witnessed with an ever anxious solicitude the violent events which have afflicted Jerusalem for many decades, and they have followed closely with watchful care the declarations of the United Nations which have dealt with the fate of the Holy City.

On many occasions the Holy See has called for reflection and urged that an adequate solution be found to this difficult and complex situation. The Holy See has done this because she is concerned for peace among peoples no less than for spiritual, historical and cultural reasons of a nature eminently religious.

The entire human race, and especially the peoples and nations who have in Jerusalem brothers in faith: Christians, Jews and Muslims, have reason to feel themselves involved in this matter and to do everything possible to preserve the unique and sacred character of the City. Not only the monuments or the sacred places, but the whole historical Jerusalem and the existence of religious communities, their situation and future cannot but affect everyone and interest everyone.

Indeed, there should be found, with good will and farsightedness, a concrete and just solution by which different interests and aspirations can be provided for in a harmonious and stable form, and be safeguarded in an adequate and efficacious manner by a special Statute internationally guaranteed so that no party could jeopardize it.

I also feel it an urgent duty, in the presence of the Christian communities, of those who believe in the One God and who are committed to the defence of fundamental human values, to repeat that the question of Jerusalem is fundamental for a just peace in the Middle East. It is my conviction that the religious identity of the City and particularly the common tradition of monotheistic faith can pave the way to promote harmony among all those who in different ways consider the Holy City as their own.

I am convinced that the failure to find an adequate solution to the question of Jerusalem, and the resigned postponement of the problem, only compromise further the longed-for peaceful and just settlement of the crisis of the whole Middle East.

It is natural in this context to recall that in the area two peoples, the Israelis and the Palestinians, have been opposed to each other for decades in an antagonism that appears insoluble.

The Church which looks at Christ the Redeemer and sees his image in the face of every man, invokes peace and reconciliation for the peoples of the land that was his.

For the Jewish people who live in the State of Israel and who preserve in that land such precious testimonies to their history and their faith, we must ask for the desired security and the due tranquillity that is the prerogative of every nation and condition of life and of progress for every society.

The Palestinian people who find their historical roots in that land and who for decades have been dispersed, have the natural right in justice to find once more a homeland and to be able to live in peace and tranquillity with the other peoples of the area.

All the peoples of the Middle East, each with its own heritage of spiritual values, will not be able to overcome the tragic events in which they are involved—I am thinking of Lebanon so sorely tried—unless they discover again the true sense of their history which through faith in the One God calls them to live together peacefully in mutual cooperation.

I desire, therefore, to draw the attention of politicians, of all those who are responsible for the destiny of peoples, of those who are in charge of International Organizations, to the plight of the City of Jerusalem and of the communities who live there. In fact, it escapes no one that the different expressions of faith and of culture present in the Holy City can and should be an effective aid to concord and peace.

On this Good Friday when we solemnly recall the Passion and Death of the Saviour, we invite you all, revered brothers in the episcopate and all priests, men and women religious, and the faithful of the whole world, to include among the special intentions of your prayers the petition for a just solution to the problem of Jerusalem and the Holy Land, and for the return of peace to the Middle East.

As this Jubilee Year of Redemption draws to a close, a year which we have celebrated with great spiritual joy whether in Rome or in all the dioceses of the universal Church, Jerusalem has been the ideal goal, the natural place to which we direct our thoughts of love and thankfulness for the great gift of the Redemption which the Son of Man accomplished for all people in the Holy City.

And since the fruit of the Redemption is the reconciliation of man with God and of every man with his brothers, we ought to pray that also in Jerusalem, in the Holy Land of Jesus, those who believe in God may find reconciliation and peace after such sorrowful divisions and strife.

This peace proclaimed by Jesus Christ in the name of the Father who is in heaven thus makes Jerusalem the living sign of the great ideal of unity, of brotherhood and of agreement among peoples according to the illuminating words of the Book of Isaiah: "Many peoples shall come and say: 'Come, let us go up to the mountain of the Lord, to the house of the God of Jacob; that he may teach us his ways and that we may walk in his paths' " (Is 2:3).

Finally we gladly impart our Apostolic Blessing.

Given in Rome at St. Peter's on Good Friday, 20 April 1984, the sixth year of our Pontificate.

To Representatives of the Jewish Community in Switzerland, Fribourg

June 14, 1984

Late in the afternoon of Thursday, 14 June 1984 the Holy Father met representatives of the Israelite Federation under the leadership of Mr. Robert Braunshweig, President of the Swiss Federation of the Israelite Community. The meeting took place in the residence of the Bishop of Fribourg. Pope John Paul II addressed the group as follows:

Dear Gentlemen and Beloved Brothers.

It is assuredly a joy for me to meet the representatives of the Swiss Federation of Jewish communities. It is always so in the course of my apostolic voyages around the world, at least whenever it is possible to do so.

I do not need to go on at length about the importance of such encounters. Making for a certain deepening of our faith and allowing us to avail ourselves of our common biblical patrimony, such encounters contribute to reducing the prejudices and even the barriers that still exist between Christians and Jews. How can Christians, on their part, remain indifferent to the problems and dangers that concern you, if not in Switzerland, at least in numerous regions of the world? From another perspective, the teaching of the Christian Churches must take into account the result of researches done with regard to this common heritage and to the foundations of Christianity in the biblical tradition. Therein lies a way towards the strengthening of our dialogue. In this regard, I am grateful to the representative of the Jewish Federation for having spoken positively about the Institute for Judeo-Christian Research at the department of Catholic theology in Lucerne.

I would also have liked, dear gentlemen and brothers, to speak with you about a fundamental problem, that of peace. The biblical *shalom*, with which it is customary to greet one another in the countries of the East, does it not contain an appeal to our responsibility? In fact, we are all invited to work ardently for the goal of peace. On its part, the Apostolic See continually endeavours to promote a peace based on justice, respect for the rights of all, and suppression of the sources of enmity, to begin with those which are hidden in the heart of man. It unceasingly advises the paths of dialogue and negotiation.

On the principle, it bears neither prejudices nor reservations towards any people. It would like to be able to manifest to all its solicitude, to aid the development of one and all, at the level of liberty, understood in its most authentic sense as on the plane of interior and exterior concord, and of the true goods capable of furthering every person and every society.

Therein lies an ideal that can be much advanced by a persevering dialogue and active and fruitful collaboration between Jews and Christians. Allow me to close this brief fraternal meeting with the salutation you like so well: *"Shalom aleijim"*. It goes out from my heart to all of you who have come to meet with me but also to your families, to the Jewish communities in Switzerland, to all of them dispersed throughout the world, and to all men of good will.

To Executive Committee of International Council of Christians and Jews

July 6, 1984

On Friday morning, July 6, 1984 in the Vatican, a delegation of the Executive Committee of the International Council of Christians and Jews was received in a 30-minute private audience by Pope John Paul II.

In his capacity as President of the ICCJ, Dr. Victor C. Goldbloom addressed the Pope on behalf of the delegation.

Remarks of Dr. Victor Goldbloom

Your Holiness,

In expressing the gratitude of the International Council of Christians and Jews for the privilege of this audience, I would like to say an introductory word to identify the ICCJ. It has existed for a considerable number of years in somewhat various forms. At present it is composed of seventeen national member organizations, all in the Western World; but it is significant that in the last four years we have been able to bring to our meetings a number of people, Christians and Jews, from Eastern Europe: from Czechoslovakia, from East Germany and from Hungary.

If we continue to meet, year after year, in this fashion, it is because of the friendship, the understanding and the trust which continue to grow between us. It is also because Anti-Semitism, and other forms of hatred, including Anti-Catholicism, are still unfortunately present in the world. But it is also because we share a sense of historic opportunity, the opportunity to set aside the antagonisms of the past and live together in peace.

For some years now, notably since (and as a result of) the Second Vatican Council, we have been experiencing a new era in Christian-Jewish relations, an era of undeniable progress.

Jews and Christians alike have reason to be grateful for the leadership which the Church has given in this work, leadership manifested by yourself and your recent predecessors; by Cardinal Bea; by Cardinal Willebrands; by Cardinal Etchegaray, whose remarkable statement we regard as a landmark and a beacon; by Msgr. Jorge Mejia, whose attendance at ICCJ meetings is greatly appreciated and whose intellectual contributions to our work are exceptionally valuable; by Dr. Eugene Fisher, both administratively and educationally; and by many, many more.

It has been a reciprocal learning process; and one of the most significant lessons we have derived from it is that the growth of harmony, understanding and mutual respect has in no way diminished the religious integrity and vitality of Judaism or of Christianity—quite the contrary—nor weakened the commitment of any Jew or of any Christian to his or her faith and tradition.

What is deeply appreciated is the readiness of the Church, under your leadership, to review liturgy, to revise catechism, to reassess and reinterpret history, to recognize that teachings and policies in the past have erected barriers and indeed led to persecutions.

What is also deeply appreciated is the sense of mutual respect and equal partnership which pervades today's relationships.

Our dialogue has become not only a conversation about Judaism and Christianity, about Jews and Christians, but also a sharing of common concerns: *for* peace, *against* violence, *against* fanaticism, *against curtailments of human rights and religious freedoms, against* injustice and inequality and discrimination, *for* cooperation and decency and human dignity. Christian-Jewish dialogue is building a foundation for working together on behalf of all humanity.

Our concern for peace extends throughout the world; it has a particular focus on the Middle East. We mourn every life that has been lost, Christian or Jewish or Muslim; and we pray that the State of Israel and its neighbours may come to live in security, in recognition, and in fruitful rather than hostile relations. We invoke your leadership towards these ends.

We renew our gratitude for the privilege of this audience. Knowing you at a distance, we have admired your courageous initiatives and have valued your contributions to Christian-Jewish understanding. Meeting you now in person, we take encouragement from you in the continuation of our work.

That encouragement emboldens us to express a particular hope. We submit with respect, and with great appreciation for the statements you have made and the positions you have taken, that it is not enough for pronouncements to be made at the highest level; they must be heard and heeded in every parish as well.

We ask you therefore to continue the leadership you have manifested in Christian-Jewish relations. We ask you, in so doing, to reinforce the work of the Vatican Commission on Relations with the Jewish People: to upgrade the Commission; to give it more scope, initiative and authority. We also hope earnestly for the day when every diocese will have a person responsible for the dissemination of new understanding among its clergy and laity, for liaison with the Jewish community wherever it exists, in the State of Israel and throughout the world, and for the educational and practical implementation, at the grass-roots level, of the statements and positions and decisions which derive from your initiative.

For all of this, we ask God's blessing upon you.

The Pope's Response

(The headline in the Vatican newspaper read: "The Pope to the International Council of Christians and Jews: The peace of the world must be built through the elimination of prejudice and the pursuit of dialogue.")

Dear Friends, Mr. President and members of the Executive Committee of the International Council of Christians and Jews,

1. I thank you, Mr. President, for the kind words of greeting with which you have now presented to me the aims, the tasks and the concerns of the International Council of Christians and Jews. And I thank you also, members of the Executive Committee, for your kindness in visiting the Pope on the occasion of your International Colloquium, to be held at Vallombrosa next week. Welcome to this house where the activities of those who promote the dialogue between Christians and Jews and are personally engaged in it are closely followed and warmly encouraged. Indeed, it is only through such a meeting of minds and hearts, reaching out to our respective faith communities, and also perhaps to other faith communities, as you try to do with Islam, that both Jews and Christians are able to profit from their "great common spiritual patrimony" (cf. *Nostra Aetate,* 4) and to make it fruitful for their own good and the good of the world.

2. Yes, a "great common spiritual patrimony" which should be, in the first place, brought to the knowledge of all Christians and all Jews and which embraces not only one or the other isolated element but a solid, fruitful, rich common religious inheritance: in monotheism; in faith in a God who as a loving father takes care of humankind and chose Abraham and the prophets and sent Jesus into the world; in a common basic liturgical pattern and in a common consciousness of our commitment, grounded in faith, to all men and women in need, who are our "neighbours" (cf. Lv 19:18a, Mk 12:32 and parallels).

This is why you are so much concerned with religious education on both sides, that the images which each of us projects of the other should be really free of stereotypes and prejudices, that they should respect the other's identity and should in fact prepare the people for the meetings of minds and hearts just mentioned. The proper teaching of history is also a concern of yours. Such a concern is very understandable, given the sad and entangled common history of Jews and Christians—a history which is not always taught or transmitted correctly.

3. There is again the danger of an always active and sometimes even resurgent tendency to discriminate between people and human groups, enhancing some and despising others. A tendency which does not hesitate at times to use violent methods.

To single out and denounce such facts and stand together against them is a noble act and a proof of our mutual brotherly commitment. But it is necessary to go to the roots of such evil, by education, especially education for dialogue. This however would not be enough if it were not coupled with a deep change in our heart, a real spiritual conversion. This also means constantly reaffirming common religious values and working towards a personal religious commitment in the love of God, our Father, and in the love of all men and women (cf. Dt 6:5, Lv 19:18, Mk 12:28-34). The golden rule, we are well aware, is common to Jews and Christians alike.

In this context is to be seen your important work with youth. By bringing together young Christians and Jews, and enabling them to live, talk, sing and pray together, you greatly contribute towards the creation of a new generation of men and women, mutually concerned for one another and for all, prepared to serve others in need, whatever their religious profession, ethnic origin or colour.

World peace is built in this modest, apparently insignificant and limited, but in the end, very efficient way. And we are all concerned for peace everywhere, among and within nations, particularly in the Middle East.

4. Common study of our religious sources is again one of the items on your agenda. I encourage you to put to good use the important recommendation made by the Second Vatican Council in its Declaration *Nostra Aetate,* 4, about "biblical and theological studies" which are the source of "mutual understanding and respect". In fact such studies, made in common, and altogether different from the ancient "disputations", tend to the true knowledge of each religion, and also to the joyful discovery of the "common patrimony" I spoke of at the beginning, always in the careful observance of each other's dignity.

May the Lord bless all your endeavours and repay you with the blessedness which Jesus proclaimed, in the tradition of the Old Testament, for those who work for peace (cf. Mt 5:9, Ps 37(36):37).

1985

To American Jewish Committee

February 15, 1985

1985 marked the anniversary of the Second Vatican Council's declaration on the Jews, "Nostra Aetate," no. 4. Consequently, there were many exchanges and colloquia not only in Rome but around the world. In the United States, for example, there were some seventy different celebrations in at least forty states. The American Jewish Committee was involved in organizing a number of these events on the Jewish side, as was the Anti-Defamation League of B'nai B'rith and other Jewish groups. This outpouring in itself, we feel, indicates the great strides that have been taken in improving relations in the years since Vatican II. The first of the Roman events was the reception of a delegation from the American Jewish Committee. The Pope took the occasion to reaffirm "Nostra Aetate" in the strongest language, language normally reserved for describing the Scriptures themselves. The talk is, thus, an important indication of the Church's ongoing commitment to the dialogue.

Statement by Howard I. Friedman
President, American Jewish Committee

Your Holiness,

It is with warm sentiments of esteem and respect that I express the heartfelt greetings of Shalom, of peace and well-being, to you on behalf of this delegation of leaders of the American Jewish Committee.

We regard this audience with Your Holiness as a particularly auspicious occasion in the history of the Catholic Church and the Jewish people. We meet with you to acknowledge the anniversaries of two climactic events:

First, 1985 marks the fortieth anniversary of the end of World War II and the defeat of the demonic ideology of Nazism whose core was racial and religious anti-Semitism. Second, 1985 commemorates the twentieth anniversary of the ending of Vatican Council II and its adoption of the historic declaration *Nostra Aetate*.

As the Nazi trauma appalled us with despair over human evil, so the 20th anniversary of the close of Vatican Council II inspires all of us with hope and promise for a more humane future. The adoption of the Vatican Declaration on Non-Christian Religions, on December 28, 1965, marked a decisive turning point in the nearly 2,000-year encounter between the Catholic Church and the Jewish people.

Nostra Aetate repudiated anti-Semitism and the infamous canard of collective Jewish responsibility for the death of Christ. It thereby rejected distorted teachings of Christian doctrine which have resulted in centuries of anti-Jewish hatred, prejudice, suffering and the prolonged shedding of Jewish blood. *Nostra Aetate* was a definitive acknowledgment by the Church of the permanent validity and legitimacy of Judaism as the authentic religious faith of the Jewish people.

We wish to acknowledge the act of justice and service to truth represented by that Declaration, and your own moving pronouncements calling for mutual respect and collaboration between Catholics and Jews in common service to humanity. It is no exaggeration to state that as a result of these far-reaching pronouncements, and the practical actions they have inspired, greater progress in improved Catholic-Jewish relations has taken place during the past two decades than in the past two millennia.

The American Jewish Committee takes special pride in this encouraging process, for we were privileged to have been intimately involved, through collaboration with the late Augustine Cardinal Bea and his Secretariat, throughout Vatican Council II. We have helped implement numerous concrete actions that have resulted in significant improvement in relations between the Catholic and Jewish peoples in the United States and in other parts of the world. Yet much remains to be done. We pledge our continued cooperation in helping further Catholic-Jewish solidarity and friendship. We sincerely hope that the forthcoming Synod of Bishops you have called will give further impetus in this direction.

As a pioneering human-relations agency, the American Jewish Committee has shared Your Holiness's vision of upholding human dignity by vigorously advocating the universality of civil and political liberties—and, in particular, religious liberty—for all peoples everywhere, especially those in oppressive totalitarian societies.

At this moment, we are actively engaged in close cooperation with Catholic Relief Services and other relief agencies in seeking to relieve the suffering, hunger and deprivation of millions of fellow human beings in Ethiopia, and in Africa generally. That life-saving collaboration between the Catholic and Jewish peoples, in service to an

64

anguished humanity, is the latest testimony to the new spirit made possible by Vatican Council II.

Your Holiness, American Jewish Committee leaders come to this Audience with you after a 10-day intensive mission in Israel. We have met with Israeli Jews, Christians and Muslims, with Palestinian Arabs, with government leaders and ordinary people. Everywhere we have found a great yearning for peace, for coexistence, for an end to conflict, violence and terrorism. We know that these goals are dear to the heart and mind of Your Holiness.

Our visit to Israel has reinforced our conviction that the primary obstacle to peace in the area is the ongoing illusion of most of Israel's neighbors that somehow, without formal recognition by other states of Israel's sovereign legitimacy, her continued existence can be undermined.

Nothing would contribute more to peace in the area than the dispelling of that illusion. That is why the extension of full recognition throughout the civilized world is so vital.

We appreciate deeply your clear grasp of that reality as expressed in your Apostolic Letter, *Redemptionis Anno*, which emphasized the Church's de facto recognition of the State of Israel and the deep ties between the Jewish people and the city of Jerusalem in these words:

> For the Jewish people who live in the State of Israel, and who preserve in that land such precious testimonies to their history and their faith, we must ask for the desired security and the due tranquility that is the prerogative of every nation and condition of life and of progress for every society . . . .
>
> Jews ardently love her [Jerusalem], and in every age venerate her memory, abundant as she is in many remains and monuments from the time of David who chose her as the capital, and of Solomon who built the Temple there. Therefore, they turn their minds to her daily, one may say, and point to her as the sign of their nation.

Your Holiness, we recognize the complexity of the problems involved, but we dare to hope that the spirit that inspired your Apostolic Letter will lead to steps that will formalize the diplomatic ties between the Holy See and the State of Israel and her people.

Such a historic act, we believe, would be a watershed event in Catholic-Jewish relations. It would help create the sense of reality which is indispensable to peace. We would consider it a happy development and confirmation of the decisions of Vatican Council II.

Above all, it would be an act of profound spiritual and ethical significance in advancing the cause of world peace.

May God bless you and strengthen the work of your hands.

Statement of the Pope

Dear Friends,

It is a great pleasure for me to receive this important delegation of the American Jewish Committee, headed by your President, and I am grateful to you for this visit. You are most welcome in this house, which, as you know, is always open to members of the Jewish people.

You have come here to celebrate the twentieth anniversary of the Conciliar Declaration *Nostra Aetate*, on the relation of the Church with non-Christian religions, the fourth section of which deals at length with the Church's relation with Judaism.

During my recent pastoral visit to Venezuela, I received some representatives of the Jewish community there, in an encounter which has now become a normal feature of so many of my pastoral visits around the world. On that occasion, in response to the greeting address of Rabbi Pynchas Brener, I said that "I wish to confirm, with utmost conviction, that the teaching of the Church proclaimed during the Second Vatican Council in the Declaration *Nostra Aetate* . . . remains always for us, for the Catholic Church, for the Episcopate . . . and for the Pope, a teaching which must be followed—a teaching which it is necessary to accept not merely as something fitting, but much more as an expression of the faith, as an inspiration of the Holy Spirit, as a word of the Divine Wisdom" (*L'Osservatore Romano*, 29 January 1985).

I willingly repeat those words to you who are commemorating the twentieth anniversary of the Declaration. They express the commitment of the Holy See, and of the whole Catholic Church, to the content of this declaration, underlining, so to speak, its importance.

After twenty years, the terms of the Declaration have not grown old. It is even more clear than before how sound the Declaration's theological foundation is and what a solid basis it provides for a really fruitful Jewish-Christian dialogue. On the one hand, it places the motivation of such a dialogue in the very mystery of the Church herself, and on the other hand it clearly maintains the identity of each religion, closely linking one to the other.

During these twenty years, an enormous amount of work has been done. You are well aware of it, since your organization is deeply committed to Jewish-Christian relations, on the basis of the Declaration, on both the national and the international levels, and particularly in connection with the Holy See's Commission for Religious Relations with Judaism.

I am convinced, and I am happy to state it on this occasion, that the relationships between Jews and Christians have radically improved in these years. Where there was ignorance and therefore prejudice and stereotypes, there is now growing mutual knowledge, appreciation and respect. There is, above all, love between us, that kind of love, I mean, which is for both of us a fundamental injunction of our religious traditions and which the New Testament has received from the Old (cf. Mk 12:28-34; Lv 19:18). Love involves understanding. It also involves frankness and the freedom to disagree in a brotherly way where there are reasons for it.

There is no doubt that much remains to be done. Theological reflection is still needed, notwithstanding the amount of work already done and the results achieved thus far. Our Biblical scholars and theologians are constantly challenged by the word of God that we hold in common.

Education should more accurately take into account the new insights and directives opened up by the Council and spelt out in the subsequent *Guidelines and Suggestions for the Implementation of "Nostra Aetate," n. 4*, which remain in force. Education for dialogue, love and respect for others, and openness towards all people are urgent needs in our pluralistic societies, where everybody is a neighbour to everybody else.

Anti-Semitism, which is unfortunately still a problem in certain places, has been repeatedly condemned by the Catholic tradition as incompatible with Christ's teaching and with the respect due to the dignity of men and women created in the image and likeness of God. I once again express the Catholic Church's repudiation of all oppression and persecution, and of all discrimination against people—from whatever side it may come—"in law or in fact, on account of their race, origin, colour, culture, sex or religion" (*Octogesima Adveniens*, 23).

In close connection with the preceding, there is the *large field of cooperation* open to us as Christians and Jews, in favour of all humanity where the image of God shines through in every man, woman and child, especially in the destitute and those in need.

I am well aware of how closely the American Jewish Committee has collaborated with some of our Catholic agencies in alleviating hunger in Ethiopia and in the Sahel, in trying to call the attention of the proper authorities to this terrible plight, still sadly not solved, and which is therefore a constant challenge to all those who believe in the one true God, who is the Lord of history and the loving Father of all.

I know also your concern for the peace and security of the Holy Land. May the Lord give to that land, and to all the peoples and nations in that part of the world, the blessings contained in the word *shalom*, so that, in the expression of the Psalmist, justice and peace may kiss (cf. Ps 85:11).

The Second Vatican Council and subsequent documents truly have this aim: that the sons and daughters of Abraham—Jews, Christians and Muslims (cf. *Nostra Aetate*, 3)—may live together and prosper in peace. And may all of us love the Lord our God with all our heart, and with all our soul, and with all our strength (cf. Dt 6:5).

Thank you again for your visit.

Shalom!

To Angelicum Colloquium on *Nostra Aetate*

April 19, 1985

The colloquium addressed here by the Holy Father was organized, on the Jewish side, by the Anti-Defamation League of B'nai B'rith and held at the Dominican House of Study in Rome, commonly known as the Angelicum. The papers from the colloquium were published in "Face to Face": An Interreligious Bulletin, published by ADL in New York.

Remarks at the Papal Audience
Rabbi Ronald B. Sobel

Your Holiness:

We of the Anti-Defamation League of B'nai B'rith have come to Rome to participate in a scholarly colloquium at the Pontifical University of Saint Thomas Aquinas, marking and celebrating the twentieth anniversary of the promulgation of *Nostra Aetate*. It is fitting and proper that we do so, not only we of the Anti-Defamation League, but the Theology Faculty at the University itself, the Friars of the Atonement, the members of SIDIC, and others both Jews and Catholic, all in cooperation with the Commission of the Holy See for Religious Relations with the Jewish People. It is altogether fitting and proper that this celebration should have taken place here in Rome within the setting of one of the more important academic institutions of the Church, for no occasion of celebration is truly worthy or inherently authentic unless joined to and accompanied by forthright, honest, dispassionate scholarship. Thus, we have come to Rome to celebrate and evaluate.

Though we are not unaware that what has transpired between the Jewish people and the Church in the past twenty years is but the beginning of a process that will lead, God willing, into the long and distant future, we are, nevertheless, fully cognizant that the past two decades have been witness to nothing less than a modern miracle, a miracle wherein within a period of one score years two thousand years of our previous relationship have been reversed. Truly, this is God's doing. In the past twenty years we His children, both Jew and Catholic, have come to realize and thus have begun to learn that theological differences, profound and decisive, need not be barriers to love and understanding; that in a world of many currents and crosscurrents Judaism and Christianity are not so much on opposite sides of the fence as we are on the same side; that though we shall never share some of the same theological convictions we do share many of the same human dreams; that though we shall probe the mystery of God each in our own way, according to the demands of our own traditions and the dictates of our own consciences, we view our world today with the same anguish and the events of our time with the same apprehension.

Your Holiness, together we see the same darkness. Together we see and understand those forces of irreligion that are addressed not to the dignity of the spirit but to the degradation of the soul. Together we share the conviction that bigotry and prejudice, born of hatred and nurtured in the failure to respect each other's commitments, can no longer be tolerated, not now, not anywhere, not at any time. Therefore, Your Holiness, we applaud with gratitude each and every one of your many pronouncements, made from here in the Vatican and elsewhere in the world, against all those demonic forces that would enslave rather than liberate, that would destroy rather than create.

It was with particular gratification, Your Holiness, that the Jewish people noted that in your Easter Message to the City and to the World, you made reference, with deep sensitivity, to the unparalleled inhumanity of Nazi brutality against the Jewish people. We shall never forget this, and it is and shall remain a source of comfort to us to know that you shall help the world to remember as well. Yesterday was Yom Hashoah, the day in our Jewish religious calendar set aside for remembrance of the Holocaust and to commemorate the martyrdom of our six million. Therefore, during our colloquium yesterday, Catholics and Jews together set aside a time to commemorate and to meditate. And in the time that we set aside, how could we forget that out of the ashes of Auschwitz rose the miracle of Israel? In and through our dialogue, we look forward to the day when Rome and Jerusalem, this Eternal City and the place where heaven touches earth, will embrace in the fullness of fraternal love and recognition.

Yes, the dialogue has begun and much has been accomplished: *Nostra Aetate* in 1965; the Guidelines for its implementation in 1974; the devoted leadership of Cardinal Willebrands, Msgr. Mejia and many others throughout the Catholic world; the work of some episcopal conferences and national commissions for relations between Christians and Jews. Much has been done, but much more needs to be done. The dialogue is not equal in all places: We continue to hear from some pulpits in Latin America echoes of the teaching of contempt; in Oberammergau we are witness to themes that have been repudiated by the Church.

But we are grateful and remain hopeful, for if we continue what we have begun it may be that history will record that thirty-three centuries after the Exodus and two thousands years after Calvary, both Christians and Jews allowed their hearts to be opened to God in new and wondrous ways.

Statement of the Pope

Dear Friends,

I am happy to greet you in the Vatican on the occasion of the Colloquium which you have called together to commemorate the twentieth anniversary of the Conciliar Declaration *Nostra Aetate*, on the relation of the Church with Non-Christian Religions, and particularly the section of it dealing with her relations with Judaism.

It is indeed a remarkable occasion, not only because of the commemoration in itself, but also because it happens to bring together Catholics, other Christians, and Jews, through the collaboration of the Theological Faculty of the Pontifical University of Saint Thomas Aquinas, the Anti-Defamation League of B'nai B'rith, the Centro Pro Unione and the "Service International de documentation judéochrétienne" (SIDIC). The Holy See's Commission for Religious Relations with the Jews has also agreed to give you its assistance and participation.

In this gathering of such important institutions for the purpose of celebrating *Nostra Aetate*, I see a way of putting into practice one of the main recommendations of the Declaration, where it says that "since the spiritual patrimony common to Christians and Jews is . . . so great, this Sacred Synod wishes to foster and recommend that mutual understanding and respect which is the fruit above all of biblical and theological studies, and of brotherly dialogues" (*Nostra Aetate*, 4).

Your Colloquium is one of those "brotherly dialogues", and it will most certainly contribute to that "mutual understanding and respect" mentioned by the Council.

Jews and Christians must get to know each other better. Not just superficially as people of different religions, merely coexisting in the same place, but as members of *such* religions which are so closely linked to one another (cf. *Nostra Aetate*, 4). This implies that Christians try to know as exactly as possible the distinctive beliefs, religious practices and spirituality of the Jews, and conversely that the Jews try to know the beliefs and practices and spirituality of Christians.

It is in this context that I note the reference in your programme to the catastrophe which so cruelly decimated the Jewish people, before and during the war, especially in the death camps. I am well aware that the traditional date for such a commemoration falls about now. It is precisely an absence of faith in God and, as a consequence, of love and respect for our fellow men and women, which can easily bring about such disasters. Let us pray together that it will never happen again, and that whatever we do to get to know each other better, to collaborate with one another and to bear witness to the one God and to his will, as expressed in the Decalogue, will help make people still more aware of the abyss which mankind can fall into when we do not acknowledge other people as brothers and sisters, sons and daughters, of the same heavenly Father.

Jewish-Christian relations are never an academic exercise. They are, on the contrary, part of the very fabric of our religious commitment and our respective vocations as Christians and as Jews. For Christians these relations have special theological and moral dimensions because of the Church's conviction, expressed in the document

71

we are commemorating, that "she received the revelation of the Old Testament through the people with whom God in his inexpressible mercy deigned to establish the ancient Covenant, and draws sustenance from the root of that good olive tree into which have been grafted the wild olive branches of the Gentiles (cf. Rom 11:17-24)" (*Nostra Aetate*, 4). To commemorate the anniversary of *Nostra Aetate* is to become still more conscious of all these dimensions and to translate them into daily practice everywhere.

I earnestly hope for this and pray that the work of your organizations and institutions in the field of Jewish-Christian relations will be ever more blessed by the Lord, whose name is forever to be praised: "Great is the Lord and highly to be praised" (Ps 145:3).

Such seems to be the proper way to dispel prejudices. But also to discover, on the Christian side, the deep Jewish roots of Christianity, and, on the Jewish side, to appreciate better the special way in which the Church, since the days of the Apostles, has read the Old Testament and received the Jewish heritage.

Here we are already in what we Christians call a *theological* field. I see in the programme of your Colloquium that you are dealing with proper theological subjects. I believe this to be a sign of maturity in our relations and a proof that the thrust and practical recommendations of *Nostra Aetate* really do inspire our dialogues. It is hopeful and refreshing to see this done in an encounter commemorating the twentieth anniversary of the Declaration.

Common theological studies cannot in fact be envisaged if there is not, on each side, a large measure of mutual trust and deep respect for each other—trust and respect which can only profit and grow from such studies.

You have also faced the question of Jewish and Christian spirituality in the present secularistic context. Yes, in our days one can sometimes have the sad impression of an absence of God and his will from the private and public lives of men and women. When we reflect on such a situation and its tragic consequences for mankind, deprived of its roots in God and therefore of its basic moral orientation, one can only be grateful to the Lord because we believe in him, as Jews and Christians, and we both can say, in the words of Deuteronomy: "Hear, O Israel, the Lord our God is one God" (Dt 6:4).

But gratitude soon turns into a commitment to express and publicly profess that faith before the world and to live our lives according to it, so that "men may see our good works and give glory to our Father who is in heaven" (Mt 5:16).

The existence and the providence of the Lord, our Creator and

Saviour, are thus made present in the witness of our daily conduct and belief. And this is one of the responses that those who believe in God and are prepared to "sanctify his name" (cf. Mt 6:9) can and should give to the secularistic climate of the present day.

A commemorative Colloquium thus easily becomes a point of departure for a new and strong dedication, not only to ever deeper relations between Jews and Christians in many fields, but also to what man needs most in the present world: a sense of God as a loving Father and of his saving will.

Address to International Catholic-Jewish Liaison Committee on the Twentieth Anniversary of *Nostra Aetate*

October 28, 1985

The twelfth meeting of the International Catholic-Jewish Liaison Committee took place on October 28-30, 1985 at the offices of the Secretariat for Promoting Christian Unity of the Holy See. The event was timed to coincide with the twentieth anniversary of the Second Vatican Council's declaration on the relationship between the Church and the Jewish people, "Nostra Aetate," no 4. That document, whose Latin title, taken from its opening words, means "In Our Times", was promulgated on October 28, 1965, by Pope Paul VI together with the 2,221 Council Fathers.

The International Liaison Committee was founded in 1970 as a means of implementing the Council's call for the institution of ongoing dialogue between the Church and the Jewish people after centuries of mistrust and often tragic conflict. The Committee is composed of representatives of the Holy See's Commission for Religious Relations with the Jews and of the International Jewish Committee for Interreligious Consultations (IJCIC). IJCIC, the International Jewish Committee for Interreligious Consultations, is composed of the World Jewish Congress, the Synagogue Council of America, the American Jewish Committee, the Israel Jewish Council for Interreligious Consultations, and B'nai B'rith.

Highlighting the event was an audience with Pope John Paul II on the afternoon of October 28th. Cardinal Johannes Willebrands, pres-

ident of the Holy See's Commission, introduced the Liaison Committee to the Pope, who has met previously with its members on earlier occasions. Rabbi Mordecai Waxman, chair of IJCIC, hailed "Nostra Aetate" and subsequent papal statements as documents which had revolutionized Christian-Jewish relations and created new opportunities for dialogue. Rabbi Waxman pointed out that the creation of the State of Israel was likewise a revolution in Jewish history which calls for new thinking by both Catholics and Jews.

The Pope, for his part, reaffirmed the Church's commitment to "Nostra Aetate" and the uniqueness of the sacred "link" between the Church and the Jewish people which he called one of "parentage, a relationship which we have with that religious community alone. . . . "

The full text of the Pope's address follows.

Dear friends,

Twenty years to the day after the promulgation of the declaration *Nostra Aetate* by the Second Vatican Council, you have chosen Rome as the venue of the 12th session of the International Liaison Committee between the Catholic Church, represented by the Holy See's Commission for Religious Relations with Judaism, and the International Jewish Committee on Interreligious Consultations.

Ten years ago, in January 1975, you also met in Rome for the 10th anniversary of the promulgation of the same document. The declaration, in effect, in its fourth section deals with the relations between the Catholic Church and the Jewish religious community. It has been repeatedly said that the content of this section, while not too long nor unduly complicated, was epoch-making and that it changed the existing relationship between the church and the Jewish people and opened quite a new era in this relationship.

I am happy to affirm here, 20 years later, that the fruits we have reaped since then, and your committee is one of them, prove the basic truth of these assertions. The Catholic Church is always prepared with the help of God's grace to revise and renew whatever in her attitudes and ways of expression happens to conform less with her own identity, founded upon the word of God, the Old and the New Testament, as read in the church. This she does not out of any expediency nor to gain a practical advantage of any kind, but out of a deep consciousness of her own "mystery" and a renewed willingness to translate it into practice. The declaration affirms, with great precision, that it is while delving into this "mystery" that she, the church, "remembers the spiritual link" between herself and "Abraham's stock".

It is this "link", which the declaration goes on to explain and illustrate, that is the real foundation for our relation with the Jewish people. A relation which could well be called a real "parentage" and which we have with that religious community alone, notwithstanding our many connections with other world religions, particularly with Islam, and which the declaration appropriately elaborates in other sections. This "link" can be called a "sacred" one, stemming as it does from the mysterious will of God.

Our relations since that historic date could only improve, deepen and branch out in different aspects and levels in the life of the Catholic Church and of the Jewish community. In this connection, as you are well aware, as far back as 1974 the Holy See took the initiative to create a Commission for Religious Relations with the Jews and also published, through that same commission, two further documents intended for the application of the declaration to many fields of the church's life: the 1975 *Guidelines* and the very recent *Notes on the Correct Way to Present the Jews and Judaism in Preaching and Catechesis in the Catholic Church.*

Both documents are a proof of the Holy See's continued interest in and commitment to this renewed relationship between the Catholic Church and the Jewish people, and to drawing from it all practical consequences.

Regarding the above-mentioned document, the *Notes* published last June, I am sure that they will greatly help toward freeing our catechetical and religious teaching of a negative or inaccurate presentation of Jews and Judaism in the context of the Catholic faith. They will also help to promote respect, appreciation and indeed love for one and the other, as they are both in the unfathomable design of God, who "does not reject his people" (Ps 94:14; Rom 11:1). By the same token, anti-Semitism in its ugly and sometimes violent manifestations should be completely eradicated. Better still, a positive view of each of our religions, with due respect for the identity of each, will surely emerge, as is already the case in so many places.

To understand our documents correctly and especially the conciliar declaration, a firm grasp of Catholic tradition and Catholic theology is certainly necessary. I would even say that for Catholics, as the *Notes* (no. 25) have asked them to do, to fathom the depths of the extermination of many million Jews during World War II and the wounds thereby inflicted on the consciousness of the Jewish people, theological reflection is also needed. I therefore earnestly hope that study of and reflection on theology will become more and more a part of our exchanges for our mutual benefit even if, quite understandably, some sections of the Jewish community may still have some reservations about such exchanges. However, deep knowledge of and respect for each other's religious identity seem essential for the reaffirmation and strengthening of the "link" the council spoke about.

The International Liaison Committee which you form is in itself a proof and practical manifestation of this "link". You have met 12 times since 1971 and despite the normal difficulties of adjustment and even some occasional tensions, you have achieved a rich, varied and frank relationship. I see here present both representatives of many local churches and of several local Jewish communities. Such large representations gathered in Rome for the 20th anniversary of *Nostra Aetate* is in itself consoling and promising. We have really made much headway in our relations.

In order to follow along the same path, under the eyes of God and with his all-healing blessing, I am sure you will work with ever greater dedication, for constantly deeper mutual knowledge, for even greater interest in the legitimate concerns of each other and especially for collaboration in the many fields where our faith in one God and our common respect for his image in all men and women invite our witness and commitment.

For the work which has been done I give thanks with you to the Lord our God, and for what you are still called to do I offer my prayers and I am happy to reaffirm the commitment of the Catholic Church to this relationship and dialogue with the Jewish community. May the Lord help your good will and your personal and institutional commitment to this important task.

Statement by Rabbi Mordecai Waxman, Chairman of the International Jewish Committee on Interreligious Consultations, during Audience with Pope John Paul II

October 28, 1985

Your Holiness,

October 28, 1965, was both a historic and revolutionary date. It marked a turning away from eighteen centuries often characterized by both misunderstanding and persecution, toward a dialogue in which we explored our common spiritual roots and confronted our disagreements frankly but in a spirit of mutual understanding and respect.

In the ensuing years, the Episcopates in the United States, Latin America and Europe have made the spirit of *Nostra Aetate* their own, carried its doctrines even further, and sought to translate them into modes of action and behaviour.

Your Holiness personally has given great depth to the dialogue and evoked a warm response from Jews and, indeed, from many Catholics throughout the world through your own statements. These included your Declaration in Mainz in 1980 in which you affirmed: "the people of God of the Old Covenant [which] was never repudiated by God. . . ." That was supplemented by your statement in Rome in 1982 that we pursue "diverse but, in the end, convergent paths with the help of the Lord."

There is a Hebrew proverb that says, *"D'vorim hayotzim min ha-lev, nichnasim el ha-lev"* ("Words which come from the heart, speak to the heart"). The warmth with which you have spoken today of our common spiritual heritage, our common concerns and our common goals enables us, in turn, to speak from the heart.

We appreciated, in *Nostra Aetate* and in the Declarations which have flowed from it, the ability of a great faith to examine itself and to chart new directions.

The repudiation of the false teachings—responsible for so much hatred and persecution—that all Jews, then and now, were responsible for the death of Jesus, encouraged Jews everywhere to feel that there was a new spirit in the Christian world. We have noted with distress, lapses from time to time into the old and repudiated language by some Catholic authorities. Nonetheless, the wide acceptance of the new approach in the Catholic world has been for us a source of hope.

The further recognition in *Nostra Aetate* and in the *Guidelines* that the Jewish religious tradition has continued to evolve and grow through the centuries to the present day and has much to contribute to our world, and the assertion that every effort must be made to understand Judaism "in its own terms," as it sees itself, made dialogue possible.

But, in these same years, the Jewish people have been undergoing a profound transformation of our own. The Nazi Holocaust shook us to the core of our being. The creation of the State of Israel restored us as a factor in history, but even more, restored us religiously and spiritually. For the third time in Jewish history, the pattern of exile and redemption was reenacted. The implications are incalculable, but we are confirmed in biblical belief that the Covenant with the Land established by the God of Abraham and his descendants endures, even as the Covenant of the Torah abides. It said to us in the words of the Torah portion read this week throughout the Jewish world that "Abraham still stands before the Lord."

We are deeply moved by the knowledge that Your Holiness has testified to this truth through your Apostolic Letter in April 1984:

> For the Jewish people who live in the State of Israel and who preserve in that land such precious testimonies to their history and their faith, we must ask for the desired security and the due tranquility that is the prerogative of every nation and condition of life and of progress for every society.

Thus, a renewed Jewish people, restored to Jerusalem and to human dignity, can engage in dialogue with the Catholic Church, confident that we have spiritual riches to cherish and to share, aware that we both have a common obligation to engage in *Tikkun Olam*— the improvement and perfecting of our world. On this anniversary of *Nostra Aetate,* we are conscious that much of its vision has yet to be translated into reality and universal acceptance. But, we look forward to the creation of structures and programs which will translate our dialogue into actions which will move the hearts of the members of our respective faiths in the joint quest for universal peace, for social justice and human rights, and for upholding the dignity of every human being created in the Divine image.

Your Holiness, in recognition of the common spiritual heritage we share and in consideration of the fact that the Catholic and Jewish worlds are commemorating the 850th anniversary of the birth of one of our greatest figures, we wish to present you with a copy of the beautiful Kaufman manuscript of the *Code of Maimonides.* With it, we offer the hope that the final line of the *Code* will be fulfilled through our continuing dialogue which shall, with God's Will, grow in depth and understanding so that "the earth may be filled with the knowledge of the Lord as the waters cover the sea."

1986

Historic Visit to the Synagogue of Rome

April 13, 1986

On Sunday, April 13, 1986, the Holy Father made his historic visit to the Synagogue in Rome. After an address of welcome by Prof. Giacomo Saban, President of the Jewish community of Rome, the Chief Rabbi Elio Toaff then spoke. In reply the Holy Father gave the following address.

Address by the Pope

Dear Chief Rabbi of the Jewish community in Rome,
Dear President of the Union of Italian Jewish communities,
Dear President of the community in Rome,
Dear Rabbis,
Dear Jewish and Christian friends and brethren taking part in this historic celebration,

1. First of all, I would like, together with you, to give thanks and praise to the Lord who stretched out the heavens and laid the foundations of the earth (cf. Is 51:16) and who chose Abraham in order to make him father of a multitude of children, as numerous "as the stars of heaven and as the sand which is on the seashore" (Gn 22:17; cf. Is 15:5)—to give thanks and praise to him because it has been his good pleasure, in the mystery of his Providence, that this evening there should be a meeting in this your "Major Temple" between the Jewish community which has been living in this city since the times of the ancient Romans and the Bishop of Rome and universal Pastor of the Catholic Church.

I likewise feel it is my duty to thank the Chief Rabbi, Professor Elio Toaff, who from the first moment accepted with joy the idea that I should make this visit, and who is now receiving me with great openness of heart and a profound sense of hospitality; and in addition to him I also thank all those members of the Jewish community in Rome who have made this meeting possible and who in so many ways have worked to ensure that it should be at one and the same time a reality and a symbol.

Many thanks therefore to you all.

Todâ rabbâ (Many thanks).

2. In the light of the Word of God that has just been proclaimed and that lives for ever (cf. Is 30:8), I would like us to reflect together, in the presence of the Holy One—may he be blessed! (as your liturgy says)—on the fact and the significance of this meeting between the Bishop of Rome, the Pope, and the Jewish community that lives and works in this city which is so dear to you and to me.

I had been thinking of this visit for a long time. In fact, the Chief Rabbi was kind enough to come and see me, in February 1981, when I paid a pastoral visit to the nearby Parish of San Carlo ai Catenari. In addition, a number of you have been more than once to the Vatican, on the occasion of the numerous audiences that I have been able to have with representatives in Italian and world Jewry, and still earlier, in the time of my predecessors Paul VI, John XXIII and Pius XII. I am likewise well aware that the Chief Rabbi, on the night before the death of Pope John, did not hesitate to go to Saint Peter's Square; and accompanied by members of the Jewish faithful, he mingled with the crowd of Catholics and other Christians, in order to pray and keep vigil, as it were bearing witness, in a silent but very effective way, to the greatness of soul of that Pontiff, who was open to all people without distinction, and in particular to the Jewish brethren.

The heritage that I would now like to take up is precisely that of Pope John, who on one occasion, as he passed by here—as the Chief Rabbi has just mentioned—stopped the car so that he could bless the crowd of Jews who were coming out of this very Temple. And I would like to take up his heritage at this very moment, when I find myself not just outside, but, thanks to your generous hospitality, inside the Synagogue of Rome.

3. This gathering in a way brings to a close, after the Pontificate of John XXIII and the Second Vatican Council, a long period which we must not tire of reflecting upon in order to draw from it the appropriate lessons. Certainly, we cannot and should not forget that the historical circumstances of the past were very different from those that have laboriously matured over the centuries. The general acceptance of a legitimate plurality on the social, civil and religious levels has been arrived at with great difficulty. Nevertheless, a consideration of centuries-long cultural conditioning could not prevent us from recognizing that the acts of discrimination, unjustified limitation of religious freedom, oppression also on the level of civil free-

dom in regard to the Jews were, from an objective point of view, gravely deplorable manifestations. Yes, once again, through myself, the Church, in the words of the well-known Declaration *Nostra Aetate* (no. 4), "deplores the hatred, persecutions, and displays of anti-Semitism directed against the Jews at any time and by anyone"; I repeat: "by anyone".

I would like once more to express a word of abhorrence for the genocide decreed against the Jewish people during the last War, which led to the *holocaust* of millions of innocent victims.

When I visited on June 1979 the concentration camp at Auschwitz and prayed for the many victims from various nations, I paused in particular before the memorial stone with the inscription in Hebrew and thus manifested the sentiments of my heart: "This inscription stirs the memory of the People whose sons and daughters were destined to total extermination. This People has its origin in Abraham, who is our father in faith (cf. Rom 4:12), as Paul of Tarsus expressed it. Precisely this People, which received from God the commandment: 'Thou shalt not kill' has experienced in itself to a particular degree what killing means. Before this inscription it is not permissible for anyone to pass by with indifference" (*Insegnamenti,* 1979, p. 1484).

The Jewish community of Rome too paid a high price in blood.

And it was surely a significant gesture that in those dark years of racial persecution the doors of our religious houses, of our churches, of the Roman Seminary, of buildings belonging to the Holy See and of Vatican City itself were thrown open to offer refuge and safety to so many Jews of Rome being hunted by their persecutors.

4. Today's visit is meant to make a decisive contribution to the consolidation of the good relations between our two communities, in imitation of the example of so many men and women who have worked and who are still working today, on both sides, to overcome old prejudices and to secure ever wider and fuller recognition of that "bond" and that "common spiritual patrimony" that exists between Jews and Christians.

This is the hope expressed in the fourth paragraph of the Council's Declaration *Nostra Aetate,* which I have just mentioned on the relationship of the Church to non-Christian religions. The decisive turning-point in relations between the Catholic Church and Judaism, and with individual Jews, was occasioned by this brief but incisive paragraph.

We are all aware that, among the riches of this paragraph no. 4 of *Nostra Aetate, three points* are especially relevant. I would like to underline them here, before you, in this truly unique circumstance.

81

The *first* is that the Church of Christ discovers her "bond" with Judaism by "searching into her own mystery" (cf. *Nostra Aetate,* ibid.). The Jewish religion is not "extrinsic" to us, but in a certain way is "intrinsic" to our own religion. With Judaism therefore we have a relationship which we do not have with any other religion. You are our dearly beloved brothers and, in a certain way, it could be said that you are our elder brothers.

The *second* point noted by the Council is that no ancestral or collective blame can be imputed to the Jews as a people for "what happened in Christ's passion" (cf. *Nostra Aetate,* ibid.). Not indiscriminately to the Jews of that time, nor to those who came afterwards, nor to those of today. So any alleged theological justification for discriminatory measures or, worse still, for acts of persecution is unfounded. The Lord will judge each one "according to his own works", Jews and Christians alike (cf. Rom 2:6).

The *third* point that I would like to emphasize in the Council's Declaration is a consequence of the second. Notwithstanding the Church's awareness of her own identity, it is not lawful to say that the Jews are "repudiated or cursed", as if this were taught or could be deduced from the Sacred Scriptures of the Old or the New Testament (cf. *Nostra Aetate,* ibid.). Indeed, the Council had already said in this same text of *Nostra Aetate,* and also in the Dogmatic Constitution *Lumen Gentium* (no. 16), referring to Saint Paul in the Letter to the Romans (11:28–29), that the Jews are beloved of God, who has called them with an irrevocable calling.

5. On these convictions rest our present relations. On the occasion of this visit to your Synagogue, I wish to reaffirm them and to proclaim them in their perennial value.

For this is the meaning which is to be attributed to my visit to you, to the Jews of Rome.

It is not of course because the differences between us have now been overcome that I have come among you. We know well that this is not so.

First of all, each of our religions, in the full awareness of the many bonds which unite them to each other, and in the first place that "bond" which the Council spoke of, wishes to be recognized and respected in its own identity, beyond any syncretism and any ambiguous appropriation.

Furthermore, it is necessary to say that the path undertaken is still at the beginning, and therefore a considerable amount of time will still be needed, notwithstanding the great efforts already made on both sides, to remove all forms of prejudice, even subtle ones, to readjust every manner of self-expression and therefore to present always and everywhere, to ourselves and to others, the true face of the Jews and of Judaism, as likewise of Christians and of Christianity, and this at every level of outlook, teaching and communication.

In this regard, I would like to remind my brothers and sisters of the Catholic Church, also those living in Rome, of the fact that the guidelines for implementing the Council in this precise field are already available to everyone in the two documents published respectively in 1974 and in 1985 by the Holy See's Commission for Religious Relations with Judaism. It is only a question of studying them carefully, of immersing oneself in their teachings and of putting them into practice.

Perhaps there still remain between us difficulties of the practical order waiting to be overcome on the level of fraternal relations; these are the result of centuries of mutual misunderstanding, and also of different positions and attitudes, not easily settled, in complex and important matters.

No one is unaware that the fundamental difference from the very beginning has been the attachment of us Catholics to the person and teaching of Jesus of Nazareth, a son of your People . . . , from which were also born the Virgin Mary, the Apostles who were the "foundations and pillars of the Church" and the greater part of the first Christian community. But this attachment is located in the order of faith, that is to say in the free assent of the mind and heart guided by the Spirit, and it can never be the object of exterior pressure, in one sense or the other. This is the reason why we wish to deepen dialogue in loyalty and friendship, in respect for one another's intimate convictions, taking as a fundamental basis the elements of the Revelation which we have in common, as a "great spiritual patrimony" (cf. *Nostra Aetate,* no. 4).

6. It must be said, then, that the ways opened for our collaboration, in the light of our common heritage drawn from the Law and the Prophets, are various and important. We wish to recall first of all a collaboration in favour of man, his life from conception until natural death, his dignity, his freedom, his rights, his self-development in a society which is not hostile but friendly and favourable, where justice reigns and where, in this nation, on the various continents and throughout the world, it is peace that rules, the *shalom* hoped for by the lawmakers, prophets and wise men of Israel.

More in general, there is the problem of morality, the great field of individual and social ethics. We are all aware of how acute the crisis is on this point in the age in which we are living. In a society which is often lost in agnosticism and individualism and which is suffering the bitter consequences of selfishness and violence, Jews and Christians are the trustees and witnesses of an ethic marked by the Ten Commandments, in the observance of which man finds his truth and freedom. To promote a common reflection and collaboration on this point is one of the great duties of the hour.

And finally I wish to address a thought to this city in which there live side by side the Catholic community with its Bishop, and the Jewish community with its authorities and its Chief Rabbi.

Let this not be a mere "co-existence", a kind of juxtaposition, interspersed with limited and occasional meetings, but let it be animated by fraternal love.

7. The problems of Rome are many. You know this well. Each one of us, in the light of that blessed heritage to which I alluded earlier, is conscious of an obligation to work together, at least to some degree, for their solution. Let us seek, as far as possible, to do so together. From this visit of mine and from the harmony and serenity which we have attained may there flow forth a fresh and health-giving spring like the river that Ezekiel saw gushing from the eastern gate of the Temple of Jerusalem (cf. Ez 47:1 ff.), which will help to heal the wounds from which Rome is suffering.

In doing this, I venture to say, we shall each be faithful to our most sacred commitments, and also to that which most profoundly unites and gathers us together: faith in the One God who "loves strangers" and "renders justice to the orphan and the widow" (cf. Dt 10:18), commanding us too to love and help them (cf. ibid. and Lv 19:18, 34). Christians have learned this desire of the Lord from the Torah, which you here venerate, and from Jesus, who took to its extreme consequences the love demanded by the Torah.

8. All that remains for me now, as at the beginning of my address, is to turn my eyes and my mind to the Lord, to thank him and praise him for this joyful meeting and for the good things which are already flowing from it, for the rediscovered brotherhood and for the new and more profound understanding between us here in Rome, and between the Church and Judaism everywhere, in every country, for the benefit of all.

Therefore I would like to say with the Psalmist, in his original language which is also your own inheritance:

hodû la Adonai ki tob
ki le olam hasdô
yomar-na Yisrael

ki le olam hasdô
yomerû-na jir'è Adonai
ki le olam hasdô (Ps 118:1–2, 4).
O give thanks to the Lord for he is good,
his steadfast love endures for ever!
Let Israel say,
"His steadfast love endures for ever".
Let those who fear the Lord say,
"His steadfast love endures for ever".
Amen.

Address by Chief Rabbi Elio Toaff

Your Holiness,

As the Chief Rabbi of this community, whose history goes back thousands of years, I wish to express to you my intense satisfaction at the gesture you have wished to carry out today, visiting a Synagogue for the first time in the history of the Church. This gesture is destined to be remembered throughout history. It shows itself linked with the enlightened teaching of your illustrious predecessor, John XXIII, who, one Sabbath morning, became the first Pope to stop and bless the Jews of Rome who were leaving this Temple after prayer, and it follows the path marked out by the Second Vatican Council, which, with the Declaration *Nostra Aetate,* produced that revolution in relations between the Church and Judaism that has made today's visit possible.

We thus find ourselves before a true turning-point in Church policy. The Church now looks upon the Jews with sentiments of esteem and appreciation, abandoning that teaching of disdain whose inadmissability Jules Isaac—may he be remembered here in blessing—brought to the attention of Pope John.

At this historic moment, my thoughts turn with admiration, gratitude and mourning to the infinite number of Jewish martyrs who serenely faced death for the sanctification of God's Name. Theirs is the merit if our faith has never wavered and if fidelity to the Lord and his Law has not failed in the long course of the centuries. Thanks to them the Jewish people lives still, the only surviving people from antiquity.

Thus, we cannot forget the past, but today we wish to begin, with faith and hope, this new historical phase, which fruitfully points the way to common undertakings finally carried out in a plane of equality and mutual esteem in the interest of all humanity.

We propose to spread the idea of the spiritual and moral monotheism of Israel in order to bring together mankind and the universe in the love, the power and the justice of God, who is the God of all, and to bring light to the minds and hearts of all men, so as to cause order, morality, goodness, harmony and peace to flourish in the world.

At the same time, we reaffirm God's universal fatherhood over all men, taking our inspiration from the prophets, who taught it as that filial love which joins all living beings to the maternal womb of the infinite as to their natural matrix. It is therefore man who must be taken into consideration; man, who was created by God in his image and likeness, with the aim of conferring upon him a dignity and nobility that he can maintain only if he wills to follow the Father's teaching. It is written in Deuteronomy, "You are children of the Lord your God", in order to indicate the relationship that must join men to their Creator, a relationship of Father and child, of love and benevolent indulgence, but also a relationship of brotherhood which must reign among all human beings. If this truly existed, we would not today have to struggle against the terrorism and twisted acts of violence that reap so many innocent victims—men, women, the elderly and children—as happened not long ago even at the threshold of this Temple.

Our common task in society should therefore be that of teaching our fellow man the duty of mutual respect, showing the iniquity of the evils afflicting the world; such as terrorism, which is the exaltation of blind and inhuman violence, and which strikes out against defenceless people, including Jews in every country, simply because they are Jews; likewise, anti-semitism and racism, which we vainly felt to be forever vanquished after the last world war.

The condemnation that the Council pronounced against every form of anti-semitism should be rigorously applied, as well as the condemnation of all violence, in order to keep all mankind from drowning in corruption, immorality and injustice.

The invitation that we read in the book of Leviticus—"I am the Lord your God; sanctify yourselves, be holy, because I am Holy"—is meant to be an exhortation to imitate the holiness of the Lord in our lives.

In this way, the image of God in potency in man from the first moment of his creation becomes the image of God in act. The "Kedoshim Tiiyu" is the imitation on the part of man of what are called the "Ways of the Lord".

In this way, by seeking to subject all their actions to the spirit, man gives the spirit dominion over material reality.

The reward for this kind of conduct is great, and God already revealed this to Abraham when he brought him out to gaze at the sky on a starry night: "I am the Lord who brought you out of Ur Casdim in order to give you possession of this land". The possession of the promised land is obtained as a reward for having followed the ways of the Lord, and the end of days will come when the people have returned there.

This return is being realized: those who escaped from the Nazi death camps have found in the land of Israel a refuge and a new life in regained liberty and dignity. It is for this reason that their return has been called by our Teachers "the beginning of the coming of final redemption", *"Reshit tzemihat geulatenu"*.

The return of the Jewish people to its land must be recognized as a good and an inalienable gain for the world, because it constitutes the prelude—according to the teachings of the prophets—to that epoch of universal brotherhood to which we all aspire, and to that redemptive peace that finds its sure promise in the Bible. The recognition of Israel's irreplaceable role in the final plan of redemption that God has promised us cannot be denied.

We will thus be able to strive together to affirm man's right to freedom, a complete freedom that encounters an inviolable boundary only when it infringes upon or limits the freedom of others. Man is born free, is free by nature, thus all men, no matter to what people they belong, must be equally free, because all have the same dignity and participate in the same rights. There are no men who can consider themselves superior and others inferior, because there is in everyone that divine spark that makes them equal.

Yet even in our own day there are still countries in the world where freedom is limited and discrimination and alienation are practised without any hesitation. I am referring in particular to blacks in South Africa, and, as far as freedom of religion is concerned, to Jews and Catholics in the Soviet Union. Our common task ought to be that of proclaiming the fact that from man's fundamental freedom there arise inalienable human rights: like the right to life, to freedom of thought, conscience and religion.

The right to life must be understood not only as the right to exist, but to see one's life guaranteed, from its birth, to see one's existence assured against every threat, every violence; it means a guarantee of the means of subsistence through a more equitable distribution of wealth, so that there are no longer people dying of hunger in the world. It means the right of each person to see his honour safeguarded, his good name against calumny and prejudice, including that of a religious nature. It means the condemnation of every attack on a person's self-respect, considered by Judaism to be equivalent to bloodshed. It means to fight against falsehood because of the disastrous consequences it can have on society, and against hate, which provokes violence and is considered by Judaism the same as hate of the Lord, of whom man is the image.

Freedom of thought also includes freedom of conscience and religious freedom. We have to strive with all our power in order to prevent man even today from being persecuted or condemned for the ideas he professes or for his religious convictions.

The concept of freedom—as we see—is a composite one, and if one of its components is suppressed, it is inevitable that sooner or later the whole complex reality of freedom will be lost, because it is a unity that has an absolute and indivisible value. It is an ideal in and of itself, one of the objects of that reign of universal justice preached in the Bible, by virtue of which men and peoples have the inalienable right to be their own masters.

Your Holiness, at this very important moment in the history of relations between our two religions, as our hearts open to the hope that the misfortunes of the past might be replaced by a fruitful dialogue that—even while respecting our existing differences—might give us the possibility of a concordant activity, of sincere and honest cooperation towards the realization of those universal ends that are found in our common roots, allow me to conclude my reflections with the words of the Prophet Isaiah: "I will greatly rejoice in the Lord, my soul shall exult in my God; for he has clothed me with the garments of salvation, he has covered me with the robe of righteousness, as a bridegroom decks himself with a garland, and as a bride adorns herself with her jewels. For as the earth brings forth its shoots, and as a garden causes what is sown in it to spring up, so the Lord God will cause righteousness and praise to spring forth before all the nations" (Is 61:10–11).

Address by Prof. Giacomo Saban

The President of the Jewish Community of Rome greeted the Holy Father with the following words.

Your Holiness,

I have the honour of being the first to welcome you to this Major Temple on the banks of the Tiber. I greet you on behalf of the most ancient Jewish Community of the Diaspora, a Community that I have been given the privilege of serving. In expressing our satisfaction at seeing a Roman Pontiff for the first time cross the threshold of a Synagogue, I feel it my duty to recount briefly the history of the Jewish

Community of this city, a history which goes back several thousand years.

Having settled on the banks of the Tiber almost two centuries prior to the destruction of the Second Temple, the fathers of the Jews that lived in Rome for centuries lived here as free Roman citizens. They wept, together with the multitude, over the mortal remains of Caesar; they applauded, together with the delirious populace, the triumph of Augustus. They were not spared, however, during the reigns of less glorious emperors, suffering, together with the rest of the inhabitants of Rome, from their wickedness and tyranny.

Their number grew with the arrival of the prisoners of the Jewish wars, and—at first slaves, but then quickly freed—they enjoyed a relatively tranquil life: witness to this fact is a stone tablet between the fourth and the fifth mile of the Ancient Appian Way. . . . But I am here speaking of the majority, because there were also those who came to Rome to ascend the glorious stairway of martyrdom, and the names of some of these are inscribed in the lists of the Mamertine Prison, from Aristobulus, son of Herod the Great, the victim of dark political designs, to Simon bar Ghiora, who fought relentlessly for our people's freedom.

Contrary to the legislation of Augustus Caesar, which, inscribed in bronze tablets and hung in the forums of the principal cities of the Empire, safeguarded the rights of our ancestors, the Theodosian Code limited their freedom, activity and development. Nonetheless, they remained—faithful to the city—perhaps the only constant component in the mosaic of populations that converged on Rome from throughout the Empire. Nor did their life consist only of trade and commerce; our commentators speak of flourishing Rabbinical academies, and many inscriptions in the catacombs witness to the fact that they constituted an inviting centre of spirituality and a source of pure monotheistic faith in the midst of a world in which paganism was moving towards its definitive extinction.

The dark centuries which followed and which saw, together with the end of the Western Empire, the decline of the city, were borne by this Community with serene courage. Shortly after the end of the first millennium, when the temporal power of the Popes was being consolidated, a son of this community, Nathan ben Jechiel Anav, whose house is found in Trastevere, not far from here, wrote in Rome the "Arukh", the first normative compendium of the Judaism of the Diaspora.

This community escaped the massacres that were inflicted upon Judaism on the other side of the Alps by croziers and Crusades; it did not, however, remain indifferent to the lot of those brothers in the faith, as is documented by the ancient funerary liturgy still in use among the Jews of Rome.

The first centuries after the year one thousand were difficult and painful for both the Jews and the rest of the population of Rome. Relations with the ruling power went through alternating phases, and violent acts were inflicted upon this Community in the persons of its Teachers. But those were the years in which Dante showed his appreciation of Immanuel Romano, who entered the world of Italian literature, bringing his metre, style and same poetic structures into Jewish literature.

The year 1492 saw the community grow with the arrival of refugees from Spain, and the liberal attitude of the Pope assured them a haven in this city.

In the following half century the situation was to change radically. In September of 1553, hundreds of copies of the Talmud were burned not far from here, in Campo di Fiori, and this blaze, which was not the first, would be re-ignited more than once in subsequent centuries. After the accession of Paul IV, with the Bull *Cum nimis absurdum* . . . of 14 July 1555, the Ghetto of Rome was established precisely where we find ourselves today. The measures introduced, harshly restrictive with regards to study and worship, as well as normal everyday activities, reduced the inhabitants of the Ghetto to economic and cultural misery, depriving them of some of their most fundamental rights.

Limitations of every sort and lack of freedom were thus the lot reserved to Roman Jews for a period of more than three centuries. It was only one hundred and fifteen years ago that this complex of restrictions, enslavement and humiliations came to cease, and not without some very sad last eruptions, such as the *"caso Mortara"* . . . .

It took more than sixty years for the Community of Rome to begin to refashion a normal existence worthy of the position that it occupies in the framework of Italian Judaism, both in terms of number and historical tradition. This process was cruelly cut short by the events immediately preceding the Second World War, with persecutions which were much more horrible in that they aimed at the complete annihilation of Judaism worldwide.

It does not fall to us to judge what took place in Rome during those years, as we are too near in time to those days. What was taking place on one of the banks of the Tiber could not have been unknown on the other side of the river, nor could what was happening elsewhere on the European continent. Nonetheless, many of our brethren found help and refuge through courageous initiatives precisely within those convents and monasteries that they had learned to fear for so many centuries.

An apostolic nuncio who would be called to the Papacy fifteen years later was not ignorant of the misdeeds that were being carried out in those days in the heart of our continent.

That Pope, John XXIII, wished to see the development of a spirituality suited to the tormented world that was finally experiencing the healing of the atrocious wounds of the war. With the Second Vatican Council he wished to give the Church an opportunity to begin anew to meditate upon fundamental values. *Nostra Aetate,* that Council document which most relates to us, introduces a different relationship between the faith of Israel and that of the surrounding world, restoring to us not only what for centuries we had been denied, but also the dignity that it had always been our right to see recognized.

The work of that "just man" has always had our praise and total appreciation; that work has been eminently carried on by his successors. That work must continue.

The efforts of men of good-will must in fact tend towards greater understanding of peoples, fully respecting their diversity. It is in this context that I feel I must manifest the aspiration to see abandoned certain reticences regarding the State of Israel. The land of Israel has a role that is central, emotionally and spiritually, in the heart of every Jew, and a change of attitude in its regard would gratify not only those present here, but Judaism worldwide. It would also, in my opinion, make a real contribution to the pacification of a region of the world that today presents threats and perils to the entire western world.

This would be a further step, then, in the *"fraternal dialogue"* of which *Nostra Aetate* speaks. I do not hesitate to believe that this step will be taken. Today's visit, Your Holiness, that you have held to be opportune—I would even say necessary—is a lively testimony to the spirit of the Council. It fills us all with joy, inasmuch as it is a sign which foreshadows better days, days in which all those who believe in the One God—may His Holy Name be blessed—will be able, united, to contribute to the creation of a better world.

"Relations with Non-Christian Religions" at General Audience

June 5, 1986

At the general audience in St. Peter's Square on Wednesday, 5 June, the Holy Father resumed his series of talks on faith and revelation after a reading from the Book of Revelation (21:23–26). While speaking of non-Christian religions in general, the Pope singled out the Church's "special relationship" with the Jewish people. The pertinent section, no. 6, follows:

6. A special relationship—with non-Christian religions—is the one that the Church has with those who profess faith in the Old Testament, the heirs of the patriarchs and prophets of Israel. The Council in fact recalls "the spiritual bond linking the people of the New Covenant with Abraham's stock" (*Nostra Aetate,* no. 4).

This bond, to which we have already referred in the catechesis dedicated to the Old Testament, and which brings us close to the Jews, is again emphasized by the Declaration *Nostra Aetate* when it refers to those common beginnings of faith, which are found in the Patriarchs, Moses and the Prophets. The Church "professes that all who believe in Christ, Abraham's sons according to faith, are included in the same patriarch's call ... the Church cannot forget that she received the revelation of the Old Testament through the people with whom God in his inexpressible mercy deigned to establish the Ancient Covenant" (*Nostra Aetate,* no. 4). From this same people comes "Christ in his human origins" (Rom 9:5), Son of the Virgin Mary, as also his Apostles are its sons.

All this spiritual heritage, common to Christians and Jews, constitutes an organic foundation for a mutual relationship, even though a great part of the children of Israel "did not accept the Gospel". Nevertheless the Church (together with the Prophets and the Apostle Paul) "awaits the day, known to God alone, on which all peoples will address the Lord in a single voice and 'serve him with one accord' (Zep 3:9)" (*Nostra Aetate,* no. 4).

Second Angelicum Colloquium

November 6, 1986

The second international Catholic-Jewish scholars' colloquium, like the first, was held at the Pontifical University of St. Thomas Aquinas (the Angelicum). The Pope's statement lists the sponsors of both colloquia. There follows here, the statement of Mr. Nathan Perlmutter, president of the Anti-Defamation League of B'nai B'rith, and then the response and welcoming statement of the Pope during his audience with the participants.

Statement of Nathan Perlmutter

Your Holiness,

We are deeply honored to again visit with you as we did when the Anti-Defamation League of B'nai B'rith joined with institutions of the Church in the commemoration of the 20th anniversary of *Nostra Aetate*.

As you know so well, modernity brings its complex challenges to individuals and to their institutions. And the Church and its children, the Synagogue and its children strive to meet these challenges. We strive to retain what has served our ancestors so well and to fashion continuity for our future generations.

The Church stands tall and proud on the foundation of Faith and Tradition. And you, your Holiness have served as its loving and inspired leader.

So too have Jews cherished Faith and Tradition. Central to Judaism is God, Torah and Israel, the Land and its people it has been central to our past, inextricably interwoven with our future.

To profess caring concern for Catholicism without respect for its faith and Tradition is to love it less. So too Jews look to their neighbors' approbation for the bedrock of their Faith, Jerusalem as the spiritual and recognized capitol of Israel.

Your Holiness, we in the ADL were deeply honored to be represented in your Day of Prayer, and Day of Peace in Assisi. How appropriate Assisi, rich in the tradition of St. Francis. Where armies have failed to bring about peace, perhaps in your example, prayer and love will facilitate peace.

The world continues to be beset by acts of terrorism, and Your Holiness knows the ravages only too well. Perhaps what is needed in addition to a Day, of Prayer for Peace, is a day in which we contemplate the evil of terrorism, and as the site for such prayers against the scourge of terrorism and war, where more appropriate than in the City of Peace, Jerusalem? And personally led by whom, more appropriately, than by your prophetic voice of peace.

Response of the Pope

Dear Friends,

1. I am very happy to welcome you on the occasion of your Second International Catholic-Jewish Theological Colloquium. In 1985 the Theological Faculty of the Pontifical University of Saint Thomas Aquinas, the Anti-Defamation League of B'nai B'rith, the Centro Pro Unione

and the "Service de Documentation Judéo-Chrétienne" (SIDIC), in cooperation with the Holy See's Commission for Religious Relations with the Jews, opened this series of theological research in commemoration of the twentieth anniversary of the Conciliar Declaration *Nostra Aetate*. According to the spirit and the perspectives of the Council, the topic chosen for your Second Colloquium, which has now come to an end, is: *Salvation and Redemption in the Jewish and Christian Theological Traditions and in Contemporary Theology*.

2. Contemplation of the mystery of universal redemption inspired the Prophet Isaiah to wonder: "Who has directed the Spirit of the Lord, or as his counsellor has instructed him? Whom did he consult for his enlightenment, and who taught him the path of justice, and taught him knowledge, and showed him the way of understanding?" (Is 40:13–14; cf. Rom 11:34). We are hereby invited to receive with humble docility the mystery of the love of God, Father and Redeemer, and to contemplate it in our heart (cf. Lk 2:51) in order to express it in our works and in our praise.

Theological reflection is part of the proper response of human intelligence and so gives witness to our conscious acceptance of God's gift. At the same time the other human sciences, such as history, philosophy and art, also offer their own contribution to an organic deepening of our faith. This is why both the Jewish and Christian traditions have always had such high appreciation for religious study. Honouring our respective traditions, theological dialogue based on sincere esteem can contribute greatly to mutual knowledge of our respective patrimonies of faith and can help us to be more aware of our links with one another in terms of our understanding of salvation.

3. Your Colloquium can help to avoid the misunderstanding of syncretism, the confusion of one another's identities as believers, the shadow and suspicion of proselytism. You are effectively carrying out the insights of the Second Vatican Council, which have also been the theme of subsequent documents of the Holy See's Commission for Religious Relations with the Jews.

This mutual effort will certainly deepen common commitment to the building of justice and peace among all people, children of the one heavenly Father. Let us, in this common hope for peace, confidently express our praise with the words of the Psalm, inviting all people to pray: "Praise the Lord, all nations! Extol him, all peoples! For great is his steadfast love toward us, and the faithfulness of the Lord endures for ever. *Hallelû-Yah* (Ps 117).

4. As I said recently in Assisi, Christians are convinced that in Jesus Christ, as Saviour of all, true peace is to be found, "peace to those

who are far off and peace to those who are near" (Eph 2:17; cf. Is 57:19; 52:7; Zec 9:10). This universal gift has its origins in the call directed to Abraham, Isaac and Jacob, and it finds its fulfilment in Jesus Christ, who was obedient to the Father even unto death on the Cross (cf. Mt 5:17; Phil 2:8). Whereas faith in Jesus Christ distinguishes and separates us from our Jewish brothers and sisters, we can at the same time affirm with profound conviction "the spiritual bond linking the people of the New Covenant with Abraham's stock" (*Nostra Aetate*, no. 4). Thus we have here a bond which, notwithstanding our differences, makes us brethren; it is an unfathomable mystery of grace which we dare to scrutinize in confidence, grateful to a God who grants us to contemplate together his plan of salvation.

Grateful for every initiative promoting dialogue between Christians and Jews, and especially for this International Catholic-Jewish Theological Co!loquium, I implore the blessing of Almighty God upon all of you and pray that your work will bear fruit for better understanding and increasing relations between Jews and Christians.

To the Jewish Community of Australia

November 26, 1986

The attitude of Catholics toward the Jewish religion "should be one of the greatest respect," Pope John Paul II told Australia's Jewish leaders November 26, 1986, in Sydney. For the Jewish people, "Catholics should have not only respect but also great fraternal love, for it is the teaching of both the Hebrew and the Christian Scriptures that the Jews are beloved of God, who has called them with an irrevocable calling." The Pope said, "no valid theological justification could ever be found for acts of discrimination or persecution against Jews. In fact, such acts must be held to be sinful." The text of the Pope's talk follows.

1. Earlier this year, I had the pleasure and privilege of visiting the synagogue in Rome and of speaking with the rabbis and the assembled congregation. At that time I gave "thanks and praise to the Lord, who stretched out the heavens and laid the foundation of the earth (cf. Is 51:16) and who chose Abraham in order to make him the father of a

multitude of children, as numerous 'as the stars of heaven and as the sand which is on the seashore' (Gn 22:17; cf. Is 15:5)."

I gave thanks and praise to him because it had been his good pleasure, in the mystery of his providence, that the meeting was taking place. Today, I praise and thank him again because he has brought me, in this great southern land, into the company of another group of Abraham's descendants, a group which is representative of many Jewish people in Australia. May he bless you and make you strong for his service!

2. It is my understanding that although the experience of Jews in Australia—an experience going right back to the beginning of white settlement in 1788—has not been without its measure of sorrow, prejudice and discrimination, it has included more civil and religious freedom than was to be found in many of the countries of the Old World. At the same time, this is still the century of the *Shoah,* the inhuman and ruthless attempt to exterminate European Jewry, and I know that Australia has given asylum and a new home to thousands of refugees and survivors from that ghastly series of events. To them in particular I say, as I said to your brothers and sisters, the Jews of Rome, "the church, in the words of the well-known declaration *Nostra Aetate,* 'deplores the hatred, persecutions and displays of anti-Semitism directed against the Jews at any time and by anyone.' "

3. My hope for this meeting is that it will help to consolidate and extend the improved relations you already have with members of the Catholic community in this country. I know that there are men and women throughout Australia, Jews and Catholics alike, who are working, as I stated at the synagogue in Rome, "to overcome old prejudices and to secure ever wider and fuller recognition of that 'bond' and that 'common spiritual patrimony' that exists between Jews and Christians." I give thanks to God for this.

4. Where Catholics are concerned, it will continue to be an explicit and very important part of my mission to repeat and emphasize that our attitude to the Jewish religion should be one of the greatest respect, since the Catholic faith is rooted in the eternal truths contained in the Hebrew Scriptures, and in the irrevocable covenant made with Abraham. We, too, gratefully hold these same truths of our Jewish heritage and look upon you as our brothers and sisters in the Lord.

For the Jewish people themselves, Catholics should have not only respect but also great fraternal love for it is the teaching of both the Hebrew and Christian Scriptures that the Jews are beloved of God, who has called them with an irrevocable calling. No valid theological justification could ever be found for acts of discrimination or persecution against Jews. In fact, such acts must be held to be sinful.

5. In order to be frank and sincere we must recognize the fact that there are still obvious differences between us in religious belief and practice. The most fundamental difference is in our respective views on the person and work of Jesus of Nazareth. Nothing, however, prevents us from true and fraternal cooperation in many worthy enterprises, such as biblical studies and numerous works of justice and charity. Such combined undertakings can bring us ever closer together in friendship and trust.

Through the law and the prophets, we, like you, have been taught to put a high value on human life and on fundamental and inalienable human rights. Today, human life, which should be held sacred from the moment of conception, is being threatened in many different ways. Violations of human rights are widespread. This makes it all the more important for all people of good will to stand together to defend life, to defend the freedom of religious belief and practice, and to defend all other fundamental human freedoms.

6. Finally, I am sure we agree that in a secularized society there are many widely held values which we cannot accept. In particular, consumerism and materialism are often presented, especially to the young, as the answers to human problems. I express my admiration for the many sacrifices you have made to operate religious schools for your children in order to help them evaluate the world around them from the perspective of faith in God. As you know, Australian Catholics have done the same. In secularized society, such institutions are always likely to be attacked for one reason or another. Since Catholics and Jews value them for the same reasons, let us work together whenever possible in order to protect and promote the religious instruction of our children. In this way we can bear common witness to the Lord of all.

7. Mr. president and members of the executive council of Australian Jewry, I thank you once again for this meeting, and I give praise and thanks to the Lord in the words of the psalmist:

Praise the Lord, all nations!
Extol him, all peoples!
For great is his steadfast
    love toward us;
And the faithfulness of the
    Lord endures for ever.
Praise the Lord! (Ps 116).